WHY SHOULD I GO TO AMSTERDAM

WHY SHOULD I GO TO ↴

AMSTERDAM

THE CITY YOU DEFINITELY
NEED TO VISIT
BEFORE YOU TURN 30

m

THIS IS WHY!

Amsterdam is a friendly city that stands for freedom, creativity, and cultural enrichment. It's a city with a soul, always surprising and renewing itself without losing its timeless character. Its compact size makes it perfect for strolling or cycling, exploring the neighbourhoods, enjoying the many museums, and experiencing the visible and palpable history. Amsterdam's international character and the many cultures living side-by-side are reflected in the numerous eating options. Looking for something to do after dinner? The city's vibrant nightlife offers endless possibilities for fun and entertainment.

Exploring this dynamic city doesn't have to break the bank. Cycle, walk, and use public transport (don't forget to jump on the free ferry!) if you don't want to miss out on the Amsterdam lifestyle. Book a nice hostel, join free tours, and visit the most beautiful sights; there is a lot to see. You don't even have to buy a ticket for the Rijksmuseum to enjoy it: the exterior, garden, and Passage alone are worth the visit. Get yourself a croquette from the famous FEBO wall or a *broodje kaas* (cheese roll), have a picnic in one of the many parks, and immerse yourself in the local culture. In short, there is always something to suit every taste and budget.

No matter the season, Amsterdam will be the cosiest village you'll ever visit. From the historic Centrum with its charming canals to the urban and industrial Noord: wherever you wander, Amsterdam is more than likely to leave a lasting impression – and a great one at that.

CONTENTS

DISTRICTS

Amsterdam may not be as large as other capitals, however, its various districts and neighbourhoods each have their own identity and features. The districts are further divided into neighbourhoods, and their names can always be found at the bottom of the street signs.

Centrum (Centre)

You'll never be bored in Amsterdam. Especially in the city centre. Its iconic canals lined with monumental buildings, the market at Waterlooplein, the canal cruises, the controversial Red-Light District; you're probably familiar with all of these even if you've never been to Amsterdam. But Centrum also boasts many other cool and slightly lesser-known spots like Noordermarkt in the Jordaan, and quieter areas like the

NOORD

XXX

CENTRUM

OOST

Oostelijke Eilanden (Eastern Islands), Haarlemmerbuurt, and hidden courtyards such as Begijnhof and Van Brienenhofje.

Noord (North)

The largest district of the city, Noord, is located across the river IJ. It has seen quite a transformation in the past few years. Previously slightly isolated, it has now been fully embraced by the rest of the city. This is partly due to the Noord/Zuidlijn, the metro line connecting the north and south since 2018, linking Noord with the rest of the city. You'll still find working-class neighbourhoods, but trendy new apartment buildings are becoming increasingly prominent. The vibe in Noord is an intriguing mixture of working-class, creative, and industrial.

Oost (East)

Amsterdam-Oost, delightfully diverse, is characterised by a mixture of students and families of different backgrounds. In Oosterparkbuurt, stately houses surround the park, while in peaceful Watergraafsmeer young families and their cargo bikes fill the streets. In Indische Buurt, over a hundred languages are spoken. On the outskirts of Oost, you'll find Bijlmer. This neighbourhood, built in the 1960s, is filled with high-rise buildings. Many Antilleans, Surinamese, and Ghanaians settled here at the time. Major attractions in the area are the Johan Cruijff Arena — Ajax's stadium — and concert halls, where music legends from around the world perform.

West

West is expansive and diverse, offering plenty to experience for a day or two. It's a very green district, with various parks such as Westerpark, the charming Erasmuspark, and Rembrandtpark. It is brimming with cool shops and restaurants, and it's a bit more laid-back than the city centre. In this district, you'll encounter plenty of impressive architecture, including the expressive *Amsterdamse School* architectural style, which was popular in the Netherlands between 1910 and 1930. At the remarkable Museum Het Schip, you can learn all about *Amsterdamse School*, art, and architecture. The residents in West are a melting pot of students, young families, and seniors, along with a mixture of many backgrounds, reflecting Dutch society as a whole.

Zuid (South)

This district is known for its tidiness and affluence. Many famous Dutch people chose to move here. It's a vibrant district with major museums located in the Museumkwartier and a high-end shopping area in P.C. Hooftstraat and Cornelis Schuytstraat. You'll need to win the lottery before you can do more than window shopping in either. In this district, you'll also find popular neighbourhood De Pijp. Once a working-class area, this is now a trendy neighbourhood that has undergone significant changes and is becoming increasingly popular. You'll find many cosy terraces, cafes, and concept stores in De Pijp. The largest park in Amsterdam can also be found in this district: the elongated Vondelpark. This park is popular with both tourists and locals. It's delightful to relax on the grass, or simply take a stroll.

PRACTICAL INFO

TRAVEL

When in Amsterdam, you'll certainly be walking. A lot. Make sure to wear comfortable shoes! Amsterdam isn't really that big, and many iconic landmarks are within walking distance of each other. But you'll cover a lot of ground anyway. Walking will always be the best way to explore a city, but there are other ways to get around.

GVB is Amsterdam's local transport provider (*gvb.nl*). Navigating the city is a breeze thanks to its extensive public transport system. In front of Central Station, you'll find both tram stops and an entrance to the metro. Buses depart from the back of the station; take the escalator upstairs to get there. The metro is very efficient, but taking a tram or bus allows you to take in some of the sights along the way.

Contactless payment can be used on all forms of public transport. Fares vary depending on the type of transport and the distance travelled. Make sure you use the same card for touching in and out throughout the day. Alternatively, you can purchase tickets at larger stations; look for the blue GVB ticket machines. On the tram and bus, only single journeys and day tickets (24 hours) are available. Multi-day tickets can be purchased at the ticket machines and service points, or the GVB phone app. Note that you cannot buy tickets on the metro; you must do so at the station before boarding.

Noord (North) and the rest of Amsterdam are divided by the IJ river. To cross it, you can use the ferry. This is both practical and fun. And it is free of charge. You can board on foot or take

a bicycle. Ferries depart from the rear of Central Station; a screen shows the time left until departure. The most frequently operating ferry goes to Buiksloterweg (every 5 minutes). It also operates at night, albeit on a reduced timetable. There are also ferries with destination IJplein and NDSM. The NDSM ferry departs from Pontsteiger (West) too. From Azartplein (Oost), a ferry sails to Zamenhofstraat (Noord).

Download the GVB app for public transport in the city and you'll always be up to date with arrival and departure times. Download the Nederlandse Spoorwegen (NS) app for train times if you're travelling to the airport or a location outside of Amsterdam. You can look up information on all Dutch transport providers (buses, trains, metros) on the app *9292 Travel Planner OV*. And of course, you can also use Google Maps.
One of the most convenient

and enjoyable ways to explore the city is by bike. Often, ho(s)tels rent out bicycles. If not, bike rental shops are abundant in the city, primarily around Central Station. Some examples are Starbikes Rental, MacBike, Black Bike, and Amsterdam Bikes.
Although we advise against it, you can drive to and through Amsterdam by car. Driving is increasingly discouraged, and parking is notoriously expensive. There are several car-free zones, and the local government plans to expand these further. If you do travel by car, we recommend parking at one of the P+R (Park and Ride) facilities, parking lots on the outskirts of the city that charge a reduced rate per 24 hours (*amsterdam.nl/en/parking/park-ride*).

From Schiphol Airport, a train departs to Amsterdam Central Station every ten minutes, and once an hour starting from 1am. You can find the train platforms in the main hall of the airport (Schiphol Plaza). Purchase a train ticket from one of the yellow ticket machines in the hall or in the NS phone-app, or you can touch in and out with your contactless debit or credit card.

Every ten minutes, bus 397 departs from bus stop B17 to the city centre of Amsterdam. This bus stops at Museumplein, Leidseplein, and Rijksmuseum, but not at Amsterdam Central Station. At night, Niteliner N97 operates to and from these stops. Download the Amsterdam Airport Express app for current schedules, and for purchasing a ticket in advance.

Taxi prices are advertised on screens at baggage claim. However, in reality, fares are much higher. We advise against taking taxis, as trains and buses are both faster and cheaper.

You can book a shared taxi to the airport, but this is not possible in the opposite direction.

WHERE TO STAY

Accommodation in Amsterdam is notoriously expensive. Youth hostels (around € 40-75 per night) are obviously cheaper than hotels (at least € 100). They often have kitchen facilities and communal areas, making them a great place to meet new people.

Hans Brinker Hostel

Kerkstraat 136-138, 1017 GR (Centrum), hansbrinker.com

Named after the imaginary boy who saved the country by plugging a hole in the seawall with his finger, this hostel is right in the city centre. Close to Leidseplein and other nightlife areas, staying here will guarantee an adventure. When the party in the city ends, the fun continues at Hans Brinker's own bar.

Heart of Amsterdam

Oudezijds Achterburgwal 120, 1012 DT (Centrum), hearthostel.nl

A hostel inspired by the world of film, with rooms themed by film classics such as *Pulp Fiction* and *American Beauty*. The perfect hostel if you want to be close to the city centre; it is located in the heart of the Red-Light District.

Durty Nelly's Inn

Warmoesstraat 115, 1012 JA (Centrum), durtynellys.nl

Highly rated hostel in the city with very comfortable bunk beds shaped like capsules, providing some privacy in the dormitory. It's clean and centrally located, the walk from Central Station is under ten minutes. Not unimportant: the showers are great!

Budget Hotel
Tourist Inn

Spuistraat 52,
1012 TV (Centrum),
tourist-inn.com

Plenty of comfort without breaking the bank, that's what characterises this hotel. Due to its location right in the city centre, it's a nice place where backpackers, students, and groups gather. Within a few minutes' walk, you can see most of the sights. Also convenient: breakfast is included in the room rates.

The Flying Pig
(uptown or downtown)

Downtown: Nieuwendijk
100, 1012 MR (Centrum),
Uptown: Vossiusstraat 46,
1071 AJ (Zuid), flyingpig.nl

Never a dull moment at The Flying Pig. Stay downtown if you're up for a wild party in their bar: it's the place to be. Stay uptown if you like to meet other travellers but also value a good night's sleep. Uptown overlooks Vondelpark, and all major museums are just around the corner.

Camping Vliegenbos

Meeuwenlaan 138, 1022
AM (Noord),
amsterdam.nl/vliegenbos

A small and peaceful campsite in a forest, still close to the free ferry and metro for easy access to the city. You can bring your own tent or rent a 'city cabin'. Fresh bread can be ordered for breakfast, and there is a small restaurant on site.

ClinkNOORD

Badhuiskade 3, 1031 KV
(Noord), clinkhostels.com

This hostel can be found in a beautiful Art Deco building dating from 1920, which alone makes staying at ClinkNOORD worthwhile. Meet fellow travellers in this cosy and clean hostel. Female-only rooms are available. Just a few minutes from the city centre, it's an enjoyable trip as you can take the free ferry to cross the IJ river.

Volkshotel

*Wibautstraat 150, 1091 GR
(Oost), volkshotel.nl*

A creative hub spanning five floors with hotel rooms, a nightclub, exhibition space, restaurant, bar, and rooftop terrace (complete with sauna and hot tubs). Enjoy fantastic views over the city from here. It's also a meeting place for locals. Book through their own website for the best pricing. The metro stops right outside Volkshotel.

Camping Zeeburg

*Zuider IJdijk 20, 1095 KN
(Oost), campingzeeburg.nl*

At the outskirts of the city, you'll find this sustainable and cosy campsite. You can rent accommodation or bring your own tent. There are communal picnic areas and various water sports activities to enjoy.

Stayokay Hostel

Zandpad 5, 1054 GA (West), Timorplein 21, 1094 CC (Oost), stayokay.com

There are two Stayokays in the city: one near Vondelpark (close to the museum area), and the other location is in Oost, with a lovely cinema around the corner. Clean, pleasant atmosphere, and a bar to boot. Public transport links are nearby, but bike rental is available too.

Train Lodge

Changiweg 121, 1043 DZ (West), trainlodge.com

Looking for a place to sleep that's both unique and comfortable? Book your bed in one of the train compartments located next to Sloterdijk station. Very friendly staff and a pleasant atmosphere. This might be our favourite place to stay in Amsterdam.

Dutchies Hostel

Sara Burgerhartstraat 21a, 1055 KV (West), dutchieshostel.com

A modern and clean hostel just outside the city centre. It offers a nice communal kitchen for those who like to do their own cooking, and there's a supermarket just around the corner. The city centre is easily accessible by public transport.

Hostel Annemarie

Jan Willem Brouwersstraat 14, 1071 LJ (West), amsterdamhostelannemarie.com

One of the cheapest places to stay in the city, so don't expect too much. But the location is perfect.

GOOD TO KNOW

Opening hours

Most supermarkets, cafes, shops, and museums are open every day, especially in the city centre. Some are closed on Sundays and Mondays, so check the website to avoid disappointment.

Alcohol & drugs

The Amsterdam nightlife, with its vibrant squares and busy streets, is always buzzing. There's a lot you can do in the liberal city of Amsterdam, but there are limits. The minimum age for buying alcohol or visiting a coffee shop is 18, make sure to always bring photo ID. Don't smoke marijuana in public; it is illegal and considered poor etiquette by Amsterdam natives. The same goes for drinking in public, for which you could get a 100 euro fine — better finish your drink before hopping to the next bar. Drugs may be offered to you on the street or in parks, but you should never engage. The quality varies hugely, and you might be putting yourself in danger.

Cycling rules

Cycling is one of the most enjoyable ways to explore the city. Cyclists rule the roads. If you're not used to this, it can be overwhelming at times. It may seem like there are no rules, and it can feel downright dangerous, but cyclists usually know exactly what they're doing. Amsterdammers cycle fast, constantly ringing their bells if they want to pass someone. You don't have to keep up with their pace but do try to maintain a reasonable speed if you cycle. Every street has a bike lane as well as a pavement: don't confuse the two. Use hand signals to indicate the direction you're going and avoid sudden stops. Use two locks for your (rental) bike. One for the front wheel attached to the frame and a secure point, and the other lock for the back.

Reservations

Just like any other big city, Amsterdam can get very crowded. As much as you might want to keep the beautiful spots to yourself, you often can't avoid other people visiting the same attractions. If you want to secure a spot in a restaurant, entry to a party, access to your favourite exhibition, or a cinema ticket, book in advance. Especially during holidays and weekends.

Card Only

Although there are plenty of cashpoints in the city, using your card for payments is often the norm. From shops to restaurants and bars, many places have an 'Alleen Pinnen' (Card-only) policy.

Tipping

There are no fixed rules for tipping in Amsterdam and the Netherlands. You simply tip if you were happy with the service or the food, with 5 to 10 percent of the bill as a norm. However, it is never mandatory.

Be respectful and careful

Amsterdam can sometimes feel like a carnival where anything goes. Don't forget that real people actually live here; they have families to keep safe and work to attend the next day. Be respectful in everything you do. Additionally, as beautiful and romantic the canals are, they can also be a death trap. Don't urinate in the canals; it's not only unpleasant but you could fall in too. There are plenty of

public urinals (*plaskrullen*) on the pavements where you can relieve yourself. These are designed for men, and we hope that more inclusive public toilets will be available soon. Getting caught for public urination will cost you at least 150 euros; enforcers are not lenient.

Red-Light District

Opinions are divided about the popular Red-Light District in the city centre. While it's one of the busiest tourist spots in Amsterdam, sex workers are simply people practising their profession. Do not take photos or videos of them; it is disrespectful and a violation of privacy. This is monitored, so don't even try to do it discreetly either.

Going places

While you may get the impression that everything is happening in the centre of town, other parts of Amsterdam are also worth your time. Turn left when everyone else goes right; it may surprise you where this could lead you. Try to get out of town too. Public transport is well organised, and distances are short: you can easily spend an afternoon visiting a nearby village or town (see page 182).

WHEN TO TRAVEL

AMSTERDAM IN SPRING

Amsterdam is simply stunning in spring. After the dark winter months, the first rays of sunshine and the rise in temperature have a huge effect on the Dutch. Everyone ventures outside, some even donning shorts when it might be a tad early, and the many terraces are bustling once again.

One of the highlights of the season is admiring the Japanese cherry blossoms in Bloesempark, located in Amsterdamse Bos. This colourful spectacle usually lasts just three weeks. Hop on a bicycle and go early to beat the crowds; it is a magical place to see the sun rise.

Spring is the perfect time to make the most of the many terraces. You'll also see lots of locals cruising along the canals; you could rent a boat and explore the city from the water. And of course, nothing beats a good picnic. Bring a blanket, grab some delicacies, and off you go. Our favourite spots are Oosterpark, Vondelpark, and Erasmuspark.

King's Day is a Dutch national holiday celebrated each year on 27th April. The party starts the night before, with crowds gathering in the streets to drink and dance the night away. On the 27th, the city transforms into one large orange-coloured flea market. Food and drinks are for sale on every street corner, and there will be live music whichever way you turn.

AMSTERDAM IN SUMMER

Oh … the Amsterdam summer! There simply is no better place. The warm summer weather is delightful in this city with its numerous swimming spots, charming terraces, and shady parks. Bring your swimwear to join the locals for a refreshing dip. Most swimming spots are easily reached, so you can go from swimming to museum in an instant. And the Dutch coast is near, so you can even plan an afternoon at the beach and take a plunge in the North Sea.

For the locals, summertime means that outdoor life unfolds. When the working day is done, people toss aside their bags to meet friends in a park, at the waterfront, or on a boat. There's always someone who knows someone who owns a boat, and everyone is welcome to join. In the mood for a barbecue? Head to the park. Do you want to spend a few hours reading your favourite book? Outside you go!

From early July to mid-September, several open-air cinemas are dotted throughout the city. Festival season is also booming in summer. Whether it's food trucks or music, or both, you can party all day long most weekends. From Latin fiesta to techno, from deep house party to canal concert: the Amsterdam summer has it all. It will be a memory to cherish forever.

AMSTERDAM IN AUTUMN

It may sound like a cliché, but sometimes clichés are simply true. Amsterdam can resemble a painting in autumn, even when it rains. With a bit of luck, you can enjoy a pleasant Indian summer in September. In parks and tree-lined streets, the foliage transitions from green to orange and yellow, creating perfect photo opportunities.

Amsterdam Dance Event, or ADE, takes place for several days in October. It is the world's biggest club festival, attracting electronic music fans from around the globe. Autumn also marks the beginning of the new cultural season, with various inspiring exhibitions opening in Amsterdam's many museums.

During this period, the city hosts *Museumnacht*, when over sixty museums open their doors in the evening and at night, offering a unique museum experience. Make sure to grab your tickets early for this popular event via *museumnacht.amsterdam.nl*. It is usually scheduled in the first half of November.

As the weather may be less favourable during this time, it might be wise to plan some indoor activities as well. Visit one of the many excellent museums, browse the shelves of one of the bookshops, or spend an afternoon vintage shopping. Don't forget to check out the IJ-hallen, and make sure to arrive early for the best finds.

AMSTERDAM IN WINTER

It doesn't get more romantic than Amsterdam in winter. In December, despite the early onset of darkness, the twinkling lights turn the city into a festive wonderland. The bridges, the old townhouses, and the streets are all adorned with lights: Amsterdam is breathtakingly beautiful during the winter season.

Rembrandtplein, a bustling hotspot, is charming with its illuminated lanterns dangling from the trees. Walk from Rembrandtplein, along one of the canals, to the illuminated Magere Brug ('Skinny Bridge'): a sight to behold. Or go on a canal cruise and admire the city from the water; it is especially enjoyable in the winter darkness. For a festive market, head to Westergasterrein.

Museumplein transforms into a winter wonderland complete with an ice rink and charming food stalls. If you've mastered ice skating and you are ready for more, head to Jaap Eden Ice Rink in Amsterdam-Oost. The locals love to skate there during the winter months. Rental skates are available, ensuring a fun time for all. If you're lucky enough to be in Amsterdam when the canals freeze over, you'll to witness many locals skating on natural ice.

Indulge in some hot chocolate or mulled wine on a terrace or in one of the bars. And don't forget to grab an *oliebol* ('oil ball'). This Dutch doughnut-type snack, traditionally eaten on New Year's Eve, is sold by many street vendors in the weeks leading up to the big night.

HISTORY

Origins of Amsterdam

Amsterdam has a rich history dating back to the 12th century. Originally founded as a small fishing village on the banks of the Amstel River, Amsterdam quickly grew into a significant trading city. The name Amsterdam is derived from the dam built in the Amstel River around 1270 to protect the city from flooding.

Trading metropolis

In the 17th century, Amsterdam flourished into a prosperous trading metropolis. The city became a major centre for trade in spices, textiles, and eventually also art and science. The canals were constructed, and the beautiful canal houses were built. These elegant buildings were once the homes of affluent merchants. A 'fun' detail is that many of these houses exhibit a characteristic curve or tilt, due to the sinking of the wooden piles in the marshy ground on which they were built. This adds to their unique character and charm, which is still preserved in the city.

Verenigde Oostindische Compagnie (VOC)

Amsterdam was a wealthy global hub, but this wealth was earned on the backs of enslaved individuals. The Verenigde Oostindische Compagnie (VOC; Dutch East India Company) played a significant role in this, as it was one of the most powerful and influential trading companies of its time. Through its extensive trade networks, the VOC facilitated the exploitation of resources and people in various parts of the world, including the Dutch colonial empire. Awareness about this part of history is increasing, and in 2023, King Willem-Alexander officially offered apologies for the role the Dutch played in the history of slavery.

Dutch painters

Over the centuries, Amsterdam has been home to numerous painters. The most famous of them all is Rembrandt van Rijn, who created *The Night Watch*. Go and see it for yourself in Rijksmuseum! Other well-known 17th century painters are Frans Hals and Johannes Vermeer. Works by painters from the Cobra movement, including Corneille and Karel Appel, can be seen at the Cobra Museum in Amstelveen. Get there in thirty minutes by bus from Museumplein.

Amsterdamse School

Amsterdam architecture is truly diverse, ranging from old canal houses to modern structures. A fine example is the *Amsterdamse School* style (1910-1930). Think sculptural shapes, stepped gables, and decorations in the façades. Iconic buildings like Scheepvaarthuis (now Amrath Hotel) and Tuschinski Theater showcase the expressionist architectural style. Key architects of this time include Michel de Klerk, Piet Kramer, and Johan van der Mey. The *Amsterdamse School* style was also used in the build of social housing for the working class; most houses can be found in Spaarndammerbuurt (West) and in Zuid.

Olympic Summer Games 1928

The 1928 Olympic Games in Amsterdam marked several historic firsts. The Olympic Stadium, built for the occasion, is still used for events and festivals. At the 1928 Games, the first Olympic flame was lit, a symbolic gesture that has since become an integral part

of the opening ceremony. Interestingly, no Olympic villages were built due to the expense; elementary schools and similar accommodations were used to house athletes instead. One of the most notable achievements came from swimmer Johnny Weissmuller, who later became known as Tarzan in the eponymous films.

Second World War

World War II was a very dark period for Amsterdam, marked by numerous cruelties deeply affecting the city and its residents. The impact of this era remains visible and palpable to this day. A large part of the Dutch Jewish community lived in Amsterdam. They had been living in the capital for centuries: it offered freedom of religion and trade, providing a safe haven for Jews who were persecuted elsewhere. This resulted in a thriving Jewish community integral to the city, mainly around Waterlooplein (Centrum), close to the synagogue. Amsterdam-Zuid also housed many Jewish families. The German occupation of the Netherlands began in May 1940. Jewish people were increasingly isolated from daily life, eventually followed by horrific mass deportations to concentration camps in 1942. Of the almost 80,000 Jews living in Amsterdam previously, only a small percentage survived the Holocaust and ultimately returned home from concentration camps like Auschwitz-Birkenau, Bergen-Belsen, and Sobibor. The post-war period was a bitter pill to swallow for those who returned. Their homes were taken over, possessions were gone, and the restitution process proceeded very slowly. This added to the immense sorrow they had endured throughout the years. In remembrance of those who fell victim to the Nazi regime, *Stolpersteine* have been laid throughout the city on pavements. The small brass-topped cubes, inscribed with the names of victims, are typically placed in front of the houses where they last resided. *Stolpersteine* are spread throughout Europe, initiated by German artist Gunter Demnig.

Anne Frank

One of the best-known stories of WWII is that of Anne Frank and her family. They went into hiding in the Secret Annex, but they were betrayed, captured, and deported to concentration camps. Only the father, Otto Frank survived and returned to Amsterdam. More on Anne on page 80.

Plantage Middenlaan

Plantage Middenlaan in Centrum-Oost was a key area during the war. Many buildings were occupied by the Nazis, like Hollandsche Schouwburg. In the former theatre, Jews were gathered before being transported. Opposite the former theatre, a Jewish daycare centre was housed; thanks to the resistance, hundreds of children and babies were saved from deportation through it. Hollandsche Schouwburg is now a monument, open daily (free of charge). Opposite the Schouwburg (no. 24), you'll find the National Holocaust Museum (no. 27), and around the corner, the National Resistance Museum (Plantage Kerklaan 61) is based. In Wertheimpark, the small park opposite the Hortus Botanicus, the National Holocaust Commemoration is held annually at the Spiegelmonument.

February Strike

The February Strike of 1941 (*Februaristaking*) was a powerful protest by Amsterdam workers against the persecution of Jews as well as the German occupation. It was sparked by the violent razzia by Nazi forces on Jonas

Daniel Meijerplein (Centrum), where hundreds of Jewish men were rounded up for deportation, triggering outrage and solidarity among the citizens. It was the only mass strike in occupied Europe against the persecution of Jews. The war lasted until 1945. On 4th May, the Netherlands commemorates the victims of WWII and on May 5th, they celebrate Liberation Day, marking the end of the occupation and the restoration of freedom and democracy.

Cultural enrichment

After the war, the city was rebuilt and significantly expanded. Old neighbourhoods underwent renovation and new neighbourhoods were constructed, such as Bijlmer in Zuidoost. The population grew rapidly as migration to the Netherlands, and especially Amsterdam, increased considerably. Migrants did not only originate from former colonies such as Suriname and Indonesia: there was also an increasing influx from countries like Spain and Italy, and later Morocco and Turkey. This migration resulted in a very diverse population as well as cultural enrichment.

Hippies & Provos

In the 1960s, Amsterdam followed another international movement: it was the era of hippies, protests, and cultural change. Protests grew rapidly with worldwide demonstrations against the Vietnam War, capitalism, and other social issues. In Amsterdam, the Provo group emerged in 1965, conducting actions against the established order. Many protests were organised around *Het Lieverdje*, a small statue on Spui, which was subsidised by the tobacco industry. According to Provos, this statue symbolised commercialised society. The protest group existed briefly but had lasting influence.

Dolle Mina's

The *Dolle Mina's* was a feminist movement founded in Amsterdam in 1970, advocating emancipation and equal rights for men and women. They organised playful weekly actions and protests to raise awareness on issues such as abortion, sexual freedom, and gender equality. Dolle Mina's broke taboos and aimed for societal change by raising awareness and exerting political pressure. Their impact was significant, contributing to the advancement of the women's movement not only in the Netherlands, but globally. A well-known protest of the Dolle Mina's was *Baas in eigen buik* ('Boss of your own belly'), drawing attention to the right to abortion and self-determination, by having the phrase written on their bellies.

Geen woning, geen kroning

On 30th April 1980, Queen Beatrix's coronation took place. However, amidst a time of extreme housing shortage (which was a problem even then) and other societal discontent, violent protests and riots erupted, with squatters clashing with the police. The slogan *Geen woning geen kroning* ('No coronation without housing') was coined during these events.

A year later, in 1981, the largest protest in Amsterdam to this date occurred, with 400,000 people taking to the streets to protest against nuclear weapons.

Freedom of speech

Protests and demonstrations, regardless of political affiliation, will always remain an integral part of Amsterdam's character and the parliamentary democracy of the Netherlands. In 2020, a Black Lives Matter demonstration was held at the Dam square, followed by COVID-19 protests in 2022 at Museumplein, and a climate march of 85,000 participants in 2023.

SIGHTSEEING

Canals

Amsterdam's iconic canals, including Herengracht, Keizersgracht, and Prinsengracht, form the city's historic ring of waterways. Each canal has its own character, lined with elegant houses, and dotted with the famously small bridges. Taking a cruise or renting a boat (see page 72) offers an unforgettable experience, showing the history and timeless allure of Amsterdam. In summer, the canals set the scene for many festivals and events.

Negen Straatjes

The Negen Straatjes ('Nine Little Streets') is an area between the Singel and Prinsengracht canals (Centrum). It consists of nine charming streets, filled with trendy boutiques, cosy cafes, and hidden gems. You can take a leisurely stroll, admire the historic buildings, and simply soak in the atmosphere. Whether you're hunting for vintage treasures or just want to relax with a cup of coffee, the Negen Straatjes have it all.

Jordaan

The Jordaan, a historic Amsterdam neighbourhood, exudes an irresistible charm. Once a working-class area, it's now a trendy district bursting with artistic flair and local character but it has been struck by gentrification as well.

Wander along the cobblestone lanes and discover eclectic boutiques, art galleries, and lively markets. We love at the Elandsgracht. Indulge in Dutch cuisine at traditional bars or savour global flavours at trendy eateries. The Jordaan also boasts cultural attractions like Anne Frank House and Westerkerk. Don't forget stopping by Monte Pelmo, one of Amsterdam's best ice cream shops (Tweede Anjeliersdwarsstraat 17).

Koninklijk Paleis

Nieuwezijds Voorburgwal 147, 1012 RJ (Centrum), paleisamsterdam.nl

The Royal Palace on the Dam, a masterpiece of Dutch 17th century architecture, is a true Amsterdam icon. Built as a city hall, it was later transformed into a royal palace. Its impressive exterior, featuring a grand classical façade and monumental columns, attracts thousands of visitors every year. Inside, you are treated to lavish rooms, richly decorated ceilings, and a stunning collection of art and furniture, reflecting the grandeur of Dutch history.

↓ PASSAGE RIJKSMUSEUM

↓ BEGIJNHOF

Amrâth Hotel

Prins Hendrikkade 108,
1011 AK (Centrum),
amrathamsterdam.com

The Amrâth Hotel is a very cool slice of history in the middle of the city. It's housed in a former shipping house, so you can imagine the amazing maritime vibe. The exterior is striking, with its Art Nouveau and *Amsterdamse School* style, and the inside is just as chic and nostalgic. A perfect blend of old-world charm and modern luxury.

Holocaust Namenmonument

Weesperstraat, 1018 DN
(Centrum),
holocaustnamen—
monument.nl

The 'Names Monument' is a tribute to the Dutch victims of the Holocaust. It consists of a labyrinth of walls engraved with the names of over 102,000 Jewish victims. Designed by Daniel Libeskind, the monument provides a space for reflection and remembrance, allowing visitors to explore the individual stories behind the names and commemorate the tragedy of the Holocaust.

Begijnhof

Begijnhof 1, 1012
WS (Centrum),
begijnhofkapelamsterdam.nl

The Begijnhof (Beguinage) located in the heart of Amsterdam, is a tranquil oasis steeped in history. Dating back to the 14th century, this charming courtyard is home to a collection of historic houses. The Begijnhof's peaceful atmosphere and picturesque gardens offer visitors a serene retreat from the bustling streets. At number 34, you'll find the city's oldest wooden house, dating back to around 1420. Open daily from 8am to 5pm.

Homomonument

Westermarkt, 1016 DV (Centrum), homomonument.nl

The Homomonument in Amsterdam stands as a powerful tribute to the LGBTQ+ community. Located near Westerkerk, it comprises three pink granite triangles symbolising past, present, and future struggles for LGBTQ+ rights. Unveiled in 1987, it's both a memorial and a living testament to the ongoing fight for equality. Visitors gather here to reflect, celebrate, and honour the diversity and resilience of the community.

Westerkerk

Prinsengracht 279a, 1016 GW (Centrum), westertorenamsterdam.nl

The recently renovated Westerkerk and its tower are an iconic presence in the city's skyline. Built in the 17th century, it's a testament to Dutch Renaissance architecture. Standing tall near Anne Frank House, the historic church tower offers panoramic views. Visitors can climb its narrow stairs to enjoy breath-taking vistas of the city below, immersing themselves in centuries of history and culture.

↓ VONDELKERK

↓ HOLOCAUST NAMENMONUMENT

Anne Frank statue

*Merwedeplein, 1078 DG
(Zuid)*

Lesser known than Anne Frank House (page 54) is the tribute to Anne Frank in Rivierenbuurt. Located in Zuid, a bronze statue of the teenager Anne stands at Merwedeplein: this is where the Frank family lived until they had to go into hiding in 1942.

Passage Rijksmuseum

*Museumstraat 1, 1071 XX
(Zuid), rijksmuseum.nl*

Even if you're not into museums, Rijksmuseum's impressive exterior is a sight to behold. Through the building tunnels the Passage, and cyclists casually ride through it on their way to work. It creates a unique urban scene. Visitors can stroll through the Passage, enjoying the architectural beauty and vibrant atmosphere of the area. You can also visit the museum gardens; they are accessible without a ticket.

Vondelkerk

*Vondelstraat 120, 1054 GS
(West)*

Vondelkerk is a stunning neogothic church-turned-event space, renowned for its striking architecture and cultural significance. Right next to Vondelpark, it hosts a variety of events, from concerts to weddings. With its grand interior, adorned with elegant stained-glass windows and ornate detailing, it is a cherished landmark and cultural venue. Its architect, Pierre Cuypers, also designed Rijksmuseum and Centraal Station. You can visit the church every first Wednesday and every third Saturday of the month, 12 noon to 4pm.

MUSEUMS

Museum Van Loon

Keizersgracht 672,
1017 ET (Centrum),
museumvanloon.nl

On Keizersgracht, you'll find this magnificent 17th-century canal house. Go there to experience the lifestyle of a regent family from that time. Wander through the many rooms, from bedroom to kitchen: everything still in its original state. Admire the artwork on the walls and stroll through the beautiful garden. Fun fact: the building's first resident was Ferdinand Bol, a pupil of painter Rembrandt van Rijn. Ferdinand Bol is now also known for something completely different, which you can read about on page 115.

Anne Frank Huis

Westermarkt 20, 1016
GV (Centrum-West),
annefrank.org

The story behind the world's most famous diary can be found in this museum. It is part of a dark chapter in history. The Jewish Frank family went into hiding in this building during World War II. They were betrayed and deported towards the end of the war. Only the father, Otto Frank returned from the concentration camps. Educational and impressive. Make sure to book well in advance.

Joods Historisch Museum / Nationaal Holocaustmuseum

Nieuwe Amstelstraat 1, 1011 PL (Centrum-Oost), jck.nl

The museum of Jewish history is located in Amsterdam's Jewish Quarter. You'll learn about the history, religion, and culture of Judaism, both in the Netherlands as a whole and in Amsterdam in particular. Additionally, you'll gain more insight into the persecution of Jews during World War II. It's a truly impressive place. Nationaal Holocaustmuseum, which opened in 2024, is a part of the museum and can be found within an eight-minute walk (Plantage Middenlaan 27).

Museum Ons' Lieve Heer op Solder

Oudezijds Voorburgwal 38-40, 1012 GD (Centrum), opsolder.nl

A truly remarkable museum, hidden in the heart of the city. This canal house served as a clandestine church in the 17th century, with 'Our Lord in the Attic' on the top floor. Almost all elements from that time have been preserved, making a visit to this museum very worthwhile. Marvel at the beautiful space and the pink colours. We love it!

↓ STEDELIJK MUSEUM

↓ FOAM

FOAM

Keizersgracht 609, 1017 DS (Centrum), foam.org

For lovers of photography. This amazing museum, along one of the canals, showcases rotating exhibitions by world-famous photographers as well as emerging young talent. It's a museum with international allure also containing a beautiful bookshop and a nice café. You can conveniently combine this museum and Museum Van Loon, as it's just a two-minute walk away.

Huis Marseille

Keizersgracht 401, 1016 EK (Centrum), huismarseille.nl

The first photography museum of the Netherlands, housed in two stately 17th century buildings. Ever changing inspiring exhibitions featuring photos that tell a story. Be sure to take a look around and admire the beautiful paintings on the ceilings, as well as other original elements of the building.

Het KattenKabinet

Herengracht 497, 1017 BT (Centrum), kattenkabinet. nl

If you're a cat person, don't miss out on the quirky, charming, and small-scale 'Cat Cabinet'. This museum pays homage to the purring quadruped with a variety of paintings, photographs, and sculptures.

Hortus Botanicus

Plantage Middenlaan 2a, 1018 DD (Centrum-Oost), dehortus.nl

From tropical to desert-like: in this botanical garden you can marvel at six thousand different tree and plant species. It's one of our favourite green spots, and it's right in the middle of the city.

Het Scheepvaartmuseum

Kattenburgerplein 1, 1018 KK (Centrum-Oost), hetscheepvaartmuseum.nl

This city (and the whole country) is inseparably connected to water, so a museum about maritime history is a must. In this beautiful building at the waterfront, you'll find 500 years of maritime history, ancient objects, and a life-sized East India Company ship. The ship is a crucial part of the museum; on it, you'll learn about the history of VOC (East India Company) ships and the colonial past.

Wereldmuseum

Linnaeusstraat 2, 1092 CK (Oost), amsterdam.wereldmuseum.nl

This World Museum, housed in a beautiful building in Oost, always links to current events in an ever-changing world. In addition to a permanent exhibition, there are many rotating exhibitions that revolve around culture, history, and diversity. The exhibitions are original, and it's often less crowded than in the museums in the centre. Tip: take a walk through neighbouring Oosterpark before or after your visit.

↓ HORTUS BOTANICUS

↓ FOAM

Van Gogh Museum

Museumplein 6,
1071 DJ (Zuid),
vangoghmuseum.nl

You can't visit the Netherlands and overlook Vincent van Gogh. Van Gogh is one of the most famous painters in Dutch art history, known for his masterpiece *Sunflowers*. In addition to showcasing his works, this museum gives an insight into the mind of the eccentric painter, and his ideas and inspirations. Not to be missed!

Rijksmuseum

Museumstraat 1, 1071 XX
(Zuid), rijksmuseum.nl

The most beautiful museum in the world? We dare to agree. You'd need more than a day to admire all the works in the impressive Rijksmuseum, which include many pieces by famous Dutch painters like Rembrandt van Rijn, Karel Appel, Johannes Vermeer, Gerard Dou, and Frans Hals. One of the highlights is Rembrandt van Rijn's gigantic *The Night Watch* at the end of the Gallery of Honour. The museum is divided by century, from the Middle Ages onwards. It also features special collections as well as a stunning library. You can take a stroll through the colourful museum garden, which is dotted with remarkable artworks and is accessible without a museum ticket.

Stedelijk Museum

Museumplein 10,
1071 DJ (Zuid),
stedelijkmuseum.nl

This museum is jokingly referred to as 'the bathtub'; take a look at its building and you'll understand. Inside is an extensive collection of modern and contemporary art. World-famous works by international and national artists such as Marlene Dumas, Piet Mondrian, Andy Warhol, and Marina Abramovic are on display.

Moco Museum

Honthorststraat 20,
1071 DE (Zuid),
mocomuseum.com

A fantastic place, in a cool villa, filled with modern art and colour. Perfect for taking the funkiest photos with you or your travel buddy as the centrepiece. Additionally, you can admire works by Banksy, Keith Haring, Damien Hirst, and other inspiring artists. It's one of few private museums in the city.

Fabrique des Lumières

Pazzanistraat 37,
1014 DB (West),
fabrique-lumieres.com

This museum offers various exhibitions of great artists from different eras, but with a twist. Works of art are digitally depicted in the large spaces of Westergasfabriek, creating an impressive experience for visitors. In Fabrique des Lumières, art is truly brought to life. It is the perfect spot for those who would like to get acquainted with classical and modern art in a whole new way.

STREET ART

Amsterdam is a great canvas for street art. Local artists enjoy using the medium to raise awareness about relevant issues, transforming it into more than just something beautiful. It is a very powerful form of expression. Street art in Amsterdam, much like in any other city, is constantly evolving. You can visit an area once and return later only to see completely different works. Downloading an app like *streetartcities* can help you in navigating the city and discovering both golden oldies and the latest artworks.

JDL street art

Artist Judith de Leeuw, aka JDL street art, is known for her huge murals the world over (Insta @jdlstreetart). She created *Our land* on the spot where her Amy Winehouse mural used to be before it was removed. *Our Land* represents the brotherhood between the Islamic, Christian, and Jewish religions in Amsterdam. The mural is applied onto an enormous sticker to prevent damage to the monumental building, although it remains technically illegal. You can find it at the corner of Vijzelgracht and Fokke Simonszstraat (Centrum), that is if it is not removed. She also created

Diversity in Bureaucracy at the corner of Kleine-Gartmanplantsoen and Leidseplein (Centrum). It depicts two Surinamese ballerinas dancing in a whirlwind of bureaucratic paperwork. The artwork comes alive when residents open their windows.

Streetart Frankey

Frank de Ruwe, aka Streetart Frankey, is known for his subtle and witty street art (Insta @ streetartfrankey). Every week, you can find one of his latest creations popping up in an unexpected place. Look out for the tiny gnome fishing for love next to the street sign of the Hartenstraat (Centrum). Or *Under Construction* at Overtoom: a Roman building is no longer missing its top,

thanks to Frankey. He also depicted former Amsterdam mayor Eberhard van der Laan in a small bronze sculpture looking down from the roof of 'Temple of Pop' Paradiso (Centrum).

STRAAT Museum

NDSM-plein 1,
1033 WC (Noord),
straatmuseum.com

This expansive museum is solely dedicated to street art and graffiti, showcasing both established and emerging names in the international street art movement. In a former shipyard, works are showcased in their grandiose glory. Most artworks were created specifically for this museum. Brazilian artist Eduardo Kobra painted a large-scale portrait of Anne Frank on the building's façade. This striking artwork, *Let Me Be Myself*, is an excellent preview of what's waiting for you inside. The museum is both educational and fun.

The Girl with the Pearl Earring

Eerste Schinkelstraat 111
(Zuid),
straatmuseum.com

In January 2024, *The Girl with the Pearl Earring*, the world-famous painting by Johannes Vermeer, was recreated by Roelof Schierbeek. It is an amazing, 117 square meter work of art.

Kamp Seedorf

NDSM-plein 1,
1033 WC (Noord),
straatmuseum.com

The art collective Kamp Seedorf has been active in the street art scene since 2010 (Insta @kampseedorf). The name refers to former footballer Clarence Seedorf, who played for Ajax as well as Real Madrid. The art collective, like Seedorf, was born in Almere. The collective consists of an unclear number of members but there is a core group of five. Apparently, they share a love for Ajax, football, graffiti, hip-hop, and beer. They have created dozens of works in both Almere and Amsterdam, including numerous murals of rappers and football players. The hand-painted paper posters are usually stuck on with glue, making them easier to remove than graffiti. That's exactly why they call their artwork 'semi-permanent'.

CINEMA

The Movies

Haarlemmerdijk 159-163, 1013 KH (Centrum), themovies.nl

Founded in 1912, this is the oldest cinema in Amsterdam. It showcases a wide variety of films, ranging from Hollywood blockbusters to arthouse productions.

Pathé Tuschinski

Reguliersbreestraat 26-34, 1017 CN (Centrum), pathe.nl

In 2021, Tuschinski was declared the most beautiful cinema in the world. For good reason! Try booking for a film screened in the main hall. You'll feel like you travelled back in time in this stunning classic theatre.

Filmtheater Kriterion

Roetersstraat 170, 1018 WE (Centrum-Oost), kriterion.nl

This popular cinema was founded in 1945, at the end of WWII, by a student resistance group. It remains a beloved spot amongst the student crowd. A great place to grab a bite and then catch a good film. Remember to bring your student ID for discounts.

Eye Filmmuseum

IJpromenade 1, 1031KT (Noord), eyefilm.nl

This impressive building at the IJ features four cinemas, an exhibition space, and an educational studio. If you linger over a drink or dinner in the bar, you'll have a beautiful view over the water. We love the location.

FC Hyena

Aambeeldstraat 24, 1021 KB (Noord), fchyena.nl

A film paradise in Amsterdam-Noord. The atmosphere is always great, and you can stay for drinks to discuss the movie afterwards, as the bar stays open until 1pm.

Studio/K

Timorplein 62, 1094 CC (Oost), studio-k.nu

A cosy cinema with a welcoming bar and restaurant in Oost, known for its wonderful arthouse films. They often offer a combo deal for film and dinner.

Lab111

Arie Biemondstraat 111, 1054 PD (West), lab111.nl

Lab111 describes itself as an eccentric cult cinema and is situated in a monumental former pathological anatomical laboratory. They offer inspiring and innovative programming.

FESTIVALS

Amsterdam boasts a vibrant festival scene year-round, with a particular buzz during the summer months. Offering diverse music genres and original venues, there's something for everyone.

FREE FESTIVALS

Amsterdam Light Festival

During December and January, beautiful light sculptures are dotted throughout the city.

amsterdamlightfestival.com

King's Day

On 27th April, the Dutch celebrate the King's birthday. Everyone dresses in orange, and celebrations take place in every bar and on every street corner. King's Night, on 26th April, is one big party too.

Bevrijdingsdag (Liberation Day)

On 5th May, the liberation of the Netherlands after World War II is widely celebrated. Many cities, including Amsterdam, organise free Bevrijdingsfestivals.

4en5meiamsterdam.nl

Rollende Keukens

Westerpark is transformed into a food paradise for a weekend in May. You can bring your own drinks.

rollendekeukens.amsterdam

Keti Koti Festival

Keti Koti, 'chains broken' in Surinamese, is celebrated on 1st July. The Dutch commemorate the abolition of slavery with a grand celebration.

ketikotiamsterdam.nl

Pride Amsterdam

This huge, inclusive event takes place in August, featuring a canal parade as well as club and street parties.

pride.amsterdam, Insta @prideamsterdam

Prinsengrachtconcert

The largest classical open-air concert in the country takes place on the Prinsengracht canal every August. Simply magical.

prinsengrachtconcert.nl

TICKETED FESTIVALS

Dekmantel

One of the most prestigious electronic music festivals world-wide, held in Amsterdamse Bos.

dekmantelfestival.com

Amsterdam Dance Event (ADE)

For one week in October, Amsterdam becomes the centre of the dance world.

Amsterdam-dance-event.nl

Milkshake Festival

A queer-friendly dance festival in Westerpark, marking the start of Pride.

Insta @milkshakefestival

International Documentary Film Festival (IDFA)

A week full of films, premieres, and talks.

idfa.nl

Thuishaven

Weekly dance festivals and parties on Saturday or Sunday, featuring both big-name and as lesser-known DJs.

thuishaven.nl

DGTL Festival

With leading names in art and electronic music, this festival takes place during Easter on the NDSM wharf.

dgtl.nl

THINGS TO DO

Tram 2

According to National Geographic, this is one of the most beautiful tram routes in the world. It takes you from Central Station past many sights.

De Balie

A debate centre providing a platform for discussions on various issues, with some events in English.
Kleine-Gartmanplantsoen 10, 1017 RR (Centrum), debalie.nl

Diamond factory

At the remarkable GASSAN Diamond factory, you can book a free guided tour and learn all about the history of diamond craftsmanship in Amsterdam.
Nieuwe Uilenburgerstraat 173-175, 1011 LN (Centrum), gassan.com/en/tours

Kuuma Sauna

A Nordic sauna experience in Amsterdam! You aim for complete relaxation first, and then jump into the canal or IJ after.
Aambeeldstraat 24, 1021 KN (Noord), kuuma.nl

Sailing through the canals

You can rent a boat (no license required) and explore Amsterdam from the water. It's more affordable when booked with a group (of other travellers).
mokumboot.nl, bootjehureninamsterdam. com, sloepdelen.nl

Open-air cinema

In summer, nothing beats watching a film under the stars. Pluk de Nacht Film Festival offers campfires and cocktails.
iamsterdam.com/uit/bioscopen-en-filmhuizen/openluchtbioscopen

Boom Chicago

This comedy club offers stand-up shows featuring established and emerging comedians alike.
Rozengracht 117, 1016 LV (Centrum), boomchicago.nl

TonTon Club Amsterdam

This arcade hall is the perfect place to enjoy some cool games, snacks, and drinks.
Polonceaukade 27, 1014 DA (West), tontonclub.nl

Fruittuin van West

During spring, you can pick your own fruit in this organic orchard, visit the shop, and relax in the garden café.
Tom Schreursweg 48, 1067 MC (West), fruittuinvanwest.nl

↓ WESTERGASTERREIN

Free Walking Tour

This organisation offers tours led by locals worldwide, including Amsterdam. You can focus on food, street art or Anne Frank, or take the classic tour and learn about the city's history, drugs policy and Red-Light District. Pay what you can.

freewalkingtoursamsterdam.com

Biking tours

When in Amsterdam, discover the city like a local and travel by bike. With a knowledgeable guide, you'll cycle along the best spots.

bajabikes.eu/nl, yellowbike.nl, mikesbiketoursamsterdam.com

Canal cruise

Cliché but fun, seeing the city's highlights by boat. Add to the fun at Blue Boat Company, with the 'Unlimited wine and cheese' offer, or take a night cruise. Boats from Rederij Kooij, a family business that has been around for over a hundred years, depart every half hour for a one-hour tour at a reasonable price. Lampedusa Tours is named after an Italian island where refugees (mainly from North Africa) arrive after a perilous boat journey. Two of those boats have been shipped to Amsterdam where they are now used for inspiring canal tours (Saturdays at 11am and 1pm). Immigrant stories, past and present, are shared along the way. Highly recommended!

Stadhouderskade 501 & 550, 1071 ZD (Zuid), blueboat.nl / Oude Turfmarkt 125, 1012 GC (Centrum), rederijkooij.nl / Dijksgracht 6, 1019 BS (Centrum), rederijlampedusa.nl

FAMOUS PEOPLE

Carice van Houten

The actress, known for her role as Melisandre in *Game of Thrones*, has appeared in both Dutch and international films such as *Valkyrie*, *Black Book*, *Race*, and *The Fifth Estate*. She also runs her own production company. She is an activist as well as an actress. She joined Extinction Rebellion and spoke out strongly against the fossil fuel industry. She is in a relationship with Australian actor Guy Pearce, whom she met on the filmset of *Brimstone*. They live in Amsterdam-Zuid with their son.

Johan Cruijff

The world-famous football player Johan Cruijff might be the most famous Amsterdammer. He passed away in 2016, but his legacy still resonates in the city. After his time with Ajax, he played for FC Barcelona and other major international clubs. His name often appears on lists of the greatest football players of all time. Cruijff grew up in a modest rental house in Betondorp (Oost), where his parents ran a small supermarket. It was on these streets that Cruijff learned to play as a young boy.

Martin Garrix

Martin Garrix, born Martijn Gerard Garritsen in Amstelveen (a municipality just outside Amsterdam), is a globally renowned DJ and music producer. Raised in a musical family, he started producing music at a young age. His breakthrough, at the age of 17(!) came with the hit *Animals* in 2013, gaining him international recognition. Garrix is known for his energetic performances and his ability to blend various music styles in his sets. He currently resides in a luxurious penthouse in Amsterdam-Zuid and remains one of the world's most sought-after DJs, with numerous hits and performances at major festivals worldwide.

Paul Verhoeven

A prolific film director celebrated for his provocative and boundary-pushing works. Renowned for his audacious storytelling and visual style, Paul Verhoeven gained international acclaim with films like *RoboCop*, *Total Recall*, *Basic Instinct*, and the Dutch production *Black Book* starring Carice van Houten. Verhoeven's fearless exploration of controversial themes and his penchant for blending genres have solidified his status as a cinematic icon. After

spending much of his career in Hollywood, he returned to the Netherlands and now resides in Amsterdam, the city where he was born in 1938. His influence on cinema extends beyond borders, shaping the landscape of filmmaking with his daring vision and unapologetic storytelling.

Famke Janssen

Famke Janssen is a versatile actress known for her powerful film and television performances. She gained international prominence as Xenia Onatopp in the Bond film *GoldenEye* (1995) and further fame as Jean Grey in the *X-Men* franchise. In addition to her acting work, she has found success both as a director and a model. With her impressive career, Janssen has made her mark on the entertainment industry and continues to inspire many, both in the Netherlands and globally. Her sisters,

Antoinette and Marjolein Beumer, are also well-known in the Dutch film industry.

Anne Frank

Anne Frank was born in Frankfurt. The Jewish girl gained worldwide fame posthumously for her *Diary of a Young Girl*. When Adolf Hitler rose to power in Germany in 1933, the Franks fled the country and settled in Amsterdam. They lived at Merwedeplein (Rivierenbuurt) in Amsterdam-Zuid. In 1942, they went into hiding in the annex of the father's business premises at Prinsengracht 263, now Anne Frank House. But in August 1944, they were betrayed, their hiding place uncovered, and the Frank family were arrested by the Gestapo. Anne ultimately died in Bergen-Belsen in early 1945, just weeks before the concentration camp's liberation. Her diary remains a poignant symbol of the Holocaust.

Their former residence on Merwedeplein is not publicly accessible but annually, a refugee writer who lacks the freedom to write in their home country is offered residency. Interested in learning more about the life of the Frank family on Merwedeplein? Historian Rian Verhoeven offers guided tours on and around the square (*annefrankwalkingtour.com*).

Freddy Heineken

Freddy Heineken was a Dutch business magnate best known as CEO of Heineken International, one of the world's largest brewing companies. Born in Amsterdam in 1923, he revolutionised the beer industry with innovative marketing strategies. He spearheaded the expansion of Heineken's global presence, making it a household name. He is also remembered for his 1983 kidnapping, which lasted for three weeks and ended with a record-breaking ransom payment of 35 million guilders. He died in 2002, leaving behind a legacy of entrepreneurship and shaping the modern beer market. Heineken's daughter, Charlene, has been the wealthiest Dutch person for years. She resides in London.

Michiel Huisman

Michiel Huisman, born in municipality Amstelveen, is a multifaced actor known for his charismatic performances in both Dutch and international productions. He rose to prominence with his role in one of the most popular soap series in the Netherlands. International recognition followed with roles in *Game of Thrones*, *Orphan Black*, and *The Haunting of Hill House*. Huisman currently lives in New York City with his family, where he continues to work on various projects.

Frank Ocean

Born as Christopher Edwin Breaux in Long Beach, California. Frank Ocean is an influential American singer-songwriter and producer. Known for his unique vocal style and introspective lyrics, his breakthrough album *Channel Orange* (2012), garnered acclaim and won him a Grammy Award. Ocean is renowned for his boundary-pushing musical style, blending influences from R&B, soul, and alternative music. Although not confirmed, rumours suggest Frank Ocean lives in Amsterdam, as he is occasionally spotted in the Dutch capital.

FILMS & SERIES
IN AND ABOUT AMSTERDAM

Amsterdamned

Amsterdamned (1988) is a thrilling Dutch film directed by Dick Maas. Set in the iconic canals of Amsterdam, it follows a detective investigating a series of gruesome murders committed by a mysterious killer lurking beneath the city's waterways. As the investigation progresses, the detective finds himself confronting not just the killer but also dark secrets hidden within the city's depths. The film combines elements of horror, suspense, and action. It offers breath-taking scenes of Amsterdam's scenic beauty juxtaposed with intense chase scenes. *Amsterdamned* remains a cult classic, celebrated for its gripping storyline, atmospheric setting, and inventive cinematography.

De Belofte van Pisa

The Promise of Pisa (2019) is a film based on the novel of the same name by Mano Bouzamour. The story is set in Amsterdam and follows Samir, a talented young man of Moroccan descent who dreams of a career in music. He finds himself at the prestigious Sweelinck Conservatorium, where he tries to prove himself in a world full of challenges and prejudice. Despite his talent and determination, Samir faces cultural conflicts, family issues, and the pressure to meet the expectations of those around him. The film explores profound themes such as identity, ambition, friendship, and cultural diversity, while tracing Samir's personal growth and quest for success and acceptance. Set against the vibrant backdrop of Amsterdam, *The Promise of Pisa* offers a touching and compelling story that is both inspiring and emotional.

Turks Fruit

Turks Fruit (Turkish Delight) is a ground-breaking 1973 Dutch film, directed by Paul Verhoeven (see page 79). Based on the eponymous novel by Jan Wolkers, it is set in 1960s Amsterdam. The film tells the story of the passionate love affair between sculptor Erik and the young, free-spirited Olga, against the backdrop of the vibrant city and the societal changes of the era. With its raw honesty, explicit scenes, and emotional intensity, *Turkish Delight* became an iconic piece of Dutch cinema. It's a tale of love, loss, and the turbulent quest for identity during a time of cultural revolution. Still iconic, and worth the watch!

De Bezette Stad

The compelling 2023 documentary *Occupied City* by British director Steve McQueen (known for *12 Years a Slave*) is partly based on a book written by his Dutch wife, Bianca Stigter, about Amsterdam during the years 1940-1945. Personal and harrowing stories from the Nazi occupation of Amsterdam are told in detail, while simultaneously showing images of the same places and houses in the present. Take your time, as the documentary has an impressive duration of four and a half hours.

Ocean's Twelve

Ocean's Twelve is a heist film from 2004 directed by Steven Soderbergh starring big names like George Clooney, Brad Pitt, and Julia Roberts. The story follows Danny Ocean and his crew as they pull off a series of elaborate heists across Europe to settle a debt. Part of the action takes place in Amsterdam, where the team faces challenges while trying to steal a valuable artifact. Amsterdam's scenic backdrop adds to the movie's appeal, providing a visually stunning setting for the characters' adventures. Including Amsterdam in the film adds an extra dose of excitement and cultural flair.

ANNE+

This series was created with the aim of producing more queer-positive film and series. The light drama series tells the story of Anne, a lesbian woman in her twenties in Amsterdam, as she searches for her place in a world where her love life and identity take centre stage. The first season, with English subtitles, is available on YouTube. Due to its success, a film was produced, which can be viewed internationally on Netflix. Check out *anneplus.nl* for more information.

Bankier van het Het Verzet

This 2018 gripping film (*The Resistance Banker*) is based on the true story of the Amsterdam banker and resistance leader Walraven van Hall (Wallie) during WWII. He, along with his brother and other members of the resistance, organised bank fraud to finance the resistance (illegal press, people in hiding, host families, and prisoners) during the Nazi regime, resulting in the largest bank fraud case in Dutch history. Opposite the Dutch National Bank (Centrum), the Walraven van Hall monument was erected on Frederiksplein in 2010.

A Small Light

This critically acclaimed biographical series (2023) is named for Miep Gies' quote "even an ordinary secretary or a housewife or a teenager can, within their own small ways, turn on a small light in a dark room." In eight episodes, the series tells the story of Anne Frank through the eyes of Miep Gies, who played a pivotal role in helping the Frank family and others take shelter in the secret annex. It sees Miep and others navigate the hazards of Nazi rule and shows the complexity of the time, being faced with the dilemma of putting yourself and others in danger for doing the right thing. A Small Light is currently streaming on Disney+.

The Hitman's Bodyguard

The Hitman's Bodyguard is a hilarious 2017 action-comedy flick starring Ryan Reynolds and Samuel L. Jackson. Reynolds plays a top-notch bodyguard tasked with babysitting Jackson, a notorious hitman, as they gallivant through Europe. They end up in Amsterdam, cruising the iconic canals and dodging bullets in the city's streets. Keep your eyes peeled for scenes shot along the charming Prinsengracht canal, adding a splash of Dutch flair to the movie's wild ride. Amsterdam serves as more than just a backdrop — it's practically a character in its own right, injecting extra excitement and laughs.

Rampvlucht

The Dutch series *Rampvlucht* (2022) revolves around the Bijlmer disaster, a plane crash in 1992 in the Bijlmer neighbourhood of Amsterdam. During this tragic event, a cargo plane from Israeli airline El Al crashed into a tower block, marking the largest air disaster ever on Dutch soil. The series follows various individuals, from residents and victims from the Bijlmer, to journalists investigating the cause of the incident. *Rampvlucht* has been sold to other countries and will be available for international audiences.

BOOKS IN & ABOUT AMSTERDAM

't Hooge Nest (The Sisters of Auschwitz) – Roxane van Iperen

One of the best-known Dutch books about World War II is Anne Frank's diary. However, the story of *The Sisters of Auschwitz* is equally remarkable. Writer Roxane van Iperen stumbled upon the story by chance. She moved with her family to a house that turned out to be a hiding place for Jews during the war. She conducted years of research and penned the extraordinary true story of the Jewish sisters Brillenslijper, who risked their lives to save others. The story partly takes place in Amsterdam, where the Brillenslijper family originated.

The Ministry of Pain – Dubravka Ugresic

The Ministry of Pain follows Tanja Lucic, a Croatian exile, and her students at the Department of Slavonic Languages in Amsterdam. As they grapple with their own traumatic pasts and the complexities of exile, they confront questions of identity, memory, and belonging. Ugresic's poignant narrative explores the psychological toll of displacement and the search for meaning in a fractured world.

Het Achterhuis (The Diary of a Young Girl) – Anne Frank

The Diary of a Young Girl is a poignant first-hand account of a Jewish girl's experiences during the Holocaust. Written while in hiding in Amsterdam, Anne Frank's diary captures her hopes, fears, and dreams amidst the atrocities of World War II. Her profound reflections on humanity, resilience, and the pursuit of normality continue to

resonate with readers worldwide, serving as a timeless testament to the human spirit.

The Fault in Our Stars – John Green

John Green's *The Fault in Our Stars* is a poignant love story set in Amsterdam. Hazel Grace Lancaster, a teenage cancer patient, meets Augustus Waters at a support group. Their shared journey to Amsterdam to meet Hazel's favourite author leads to a profound exploration of life, love, and mortality in the city's picturesque backdrop.

The Fall – Albert Camus

A philosophical novel set in Amsterdam. *The Fall*'s protagonist, Jean-Baptiste Clamence, confesses his sins to a stranger in a bar. Through his existential reflections, Camus explores themes of guilt, morality, and the human condition against the backdrop of the city's atmospheric canals and streets.

Een kleine geschiedenis van Amsterdam (Amsterdam: A Brief Life of the City) – Geert Mak

Geert Mak's *A Brief Life of the City* takes you on a captivating journey through the rich history of the Dutch capital. From its humble origins as a fishing village to its rise as a world-renowned trading city, Mak reveals the fascinating stories behind the iconic canals, buildings, and people that shaped Amsterdam. Geert Mak is a renowned Dutch author who specialises in history and Europe.

The Goldfinch – Donna Tartt

The Goldfinch by Donna Tartt is a gripping novel set in Amsterdam as well as other cities. Surviving a tragic event, Theo Decker becomes entangled in the underworld of art theft. As he navigates loss, love, and betrayal, the iconic canals and historic streets of Amsterdam provide a backdrop to his tumultuous journey.

My 'Dam Life: three years in Holland – Sean Condon

Get ready to dive into the hilariously chaotic world of Amsterdam expat life with Sean Condon's memoir, *My 'Dam Life*. With humour and insight, Condon navigates the city's quirks and eccentricities, offering a candid portrayal of expat life in the Dutch capital while providing entertaining anecdotes and observations.

The Miniaturist – Jessie Burton

The Miniaturist by Jessie Burton is a bestselling novel set in 17th-century Amsterdam. When Nella Oortman arrives at her new husband's home, she receives a mysterious dollhouse replica of their house. As she uncovers its secrets, she delves into the city's opulent yet secretive world, leading to unexpected revelations.

The light of Amsterdam – David Park

Set against the backdrop of Amsterdam's bustling streets and illuminated nightscapes, *The Light of Amsterdam* by David Park unfolds over the course of one weekend, intertwining the lives of three characters as they navigate personal struggles and desires.

FUN FACTS

Government

Although it is the capital, the Dutch government doesn't hold seat in Amsterdam. Originally, the country was divided into small states, run by noblemen with differing stakes. They eventually held their meetings in The Hague, a town of no real significance at the time, making it neutral ground. After the foundation of the Kingdom of the Netherlands and the following split from Belgium, King Willem declared Amsterdam its capital, as it was the main trade city. The Hague, however, remained the permanent seat of government.

Mokum

Amsterdam is nicknamed Mokum, which stems from *mokem*, the Yiddish word for 'place' or 'city'. During the 17th century, Mokum was considered a safe haven for European Jews.

Super tiny house

The smallest house in Europe can be found in Amsterdam, at Oude Hoogstraat 22 (Centrum). It is approximately two meters wide and five meters deep, and a fine miniature example of an Amsterdam canal house.

XXX

The XXX symbol can be seen on Amsterdam's flag, as well as all over town, carved on buildings, into bollards, and stamped on official letters. Its origin is unclear. There are many theories on the subject. Despite Amsterdam's reputation, there is no relation to the X in X-rated. Some say it's representative of St. Andrew, Jesus' Apostle crucified on an X-shaped cross. Another theory is that the three crosses represent the three dangers of Old Amsterdam: fire, floods, and the Black Death. And then some say it represents the three kisses the Dutch plant on each other's cheeks as a form of greeting.

Same-sex marriages

On 1st April 2001, the Netherlands became the first country in the world to legalise same-sex marriages. On that day, the Amsterdam mayor married four couples, just after midnight. Over twenty-five countries followed the example since.

Venice of the North

Due to its canals and bridges, Amsterdam is also known as 'Venice of the North'. Counting over 1,800 bridges, Amsterdam even beats Venice, with its 400 bridges.

Canal Ring

Amsterdam's 165 canals separate the city into ninety different islands. The historic canal ring is now a UNESCO World Heritage site.

Houseboats

Amsterdam canals are lined with hundreds of houseboats. Most are residential, some house hotels or museums. And then there's the *Poezenboot* or the 'Cat Boat'. This floating cat sanctuary takes in 250 strays every year. You can visit this unique cat shelter during visitor hours (*depoezenboot.nl/ en*).

Plaskrul

The first Plaskrul ('Pee Curl') was placed in Amsterdam around 1870. The unique curved design, containing perforated metal, allows for privacy while simultaneously offering a view inside. It is designed to prevent public urinating. These constructions are slowly disappearing, making way for more inclusive designs.

Bicycles

In Amsterdam, there are four times more bicycles than there are cars, since cycling is easy and quick for getting around the central part of town. There are nearly a million bikes in Amsterdam alone. As many as 15,000 bikes are fished out of the canals each year, with a boat sailing around fishing for bicycles!

Moving by bike

Don't be surprised to see people transporting all their belongings in a cargo bike. Within the student community, this is a great way to move house; you can rent cargo bikes especially for this purpose.

Yiddish vocab used in Dutch

As a large Jewish community formed in Amsterdam from the 17th century, many Yiddish words became part of the city's vocabulary, eventually entering the Dutch language throughout the Netherlands. Some examples:

- *gabber* – friend (from *chaver*)
- *lef* – guts, courage (from *lev*, meaning 'heart')
- *mazzel* – fortune (from the word *mazal*)
- *sores* – trouble (from *tsarot*)
- *stiekem* – secretly (from *shtika*, meaning 'silence')
- *tof* – great (from *tov*)

PHOTO SPOTS

Magere brug

*Between Kerkstraat &
Nieuwe Kerkstraat, 1018
EG (Centrum)*

The 'Skinny Bridge' is an iconic Amsterdam photo spot due to its charm, historical significance, and beautiful location over the Amstel. Originally built in the 17th century with a narrow passage for ships, the bridge owes its name to its slender design. The bridge's lights create a romantic atmosphere in the evening, reflecting beautifully in the calm waters. Surrounded by historical canal houses, the Magere Brug remains an essential stop for every budding photographer.

De Dam

One of the most popular and bustling spots in the city is de Dam (Centrum). If you come early, during sunrise (in the summer months from 5.30am), it seems like a different place altogether. The morning light shines along and in between the buildings and through streets, with department store De Bijenkorf and the Royal Palace completely still. We also recommend walking from Damrak to Central Station at that time of day, we love it. Besides a few pigeons and other early birds, you'll have the city to yourself.

↓ NDSM

↓ REM-EILAND

NEMO Science Museum

Oosterdok 2, 1011 VX (Centrum), nemosciencemuseum.nl

Visit the rooftop of the science museum and enjoy stunning views over the water and the city beyond. Perfect for capturing beautiful shots. Great for some relaxation too, as there is plenty of seating available. It opens daily from 10am to 5.30pm, and it has free access via the stairs on the east side of the building.

Weesperzijde

The Amstel River runs through the city. The road parallel to it on the east is Weesperzijde. Here, beautiful houses line the waterfront. Even more wonderful in spring when abundant wisteria adorns the houses. Start at De Ysbreeker restaurant and walk along Weesperzijde until you can't go any further. It takes about half an hour; depending on the amount of photo stops you make, of course.

Canals

Obviously, the canals cannot be missed from this list. The countless canals serve as beautiful backdrops. Each with its own charm with the bikes parked on the bridges, the flowers, and the passing boats. We recommend Reguliersgracht (between Keizersgracht and Prinsengracht), and Bloemgracht on the west side of the canal ring. But the truth is that everything in between offers a beautiful setting too.

NDSM

NDSM-Plein 28,
1033 WB (Noord)

The NDSM wharf, with its cool industrial vibe and artistic flair, is a fantastic spot for some snaps. It's like a massive open-air art gallery with colourful graffiti and unique installations on old shipyard cranes. You'll also find rugged, abandoned buildings and ship docks that exude a raw beauty. The contrast between the old industrial area and the modern art makes it a great backdrop for your urban shots. Doesn't matter if you're a pro or not, the wharf offers endless opportunities for uniquely vibrant photos.

A'DAM LOOKOUT

Overhoeksplein 5, 1031 KS
(Noord),
adamlookout.com

The highest swing in Europe. Experience Amsterdam from 100 meters above ground on the rooftop of the A'dam Tower in Noord. Not recommended if you have a fear of heights.

REM-Eiland

Haparandadam 45-2,
1013 AK (West),
remeiland.nl

Formerly, a platform in the North Sea used for broadcasting commercial radio and television. In 2011, the platform was relocated to the Houthavens (West). It now houses a restaurant, bar, and rooftop terrace. The restaurant might be out of your price range, but a drink on the rooftop terrace will give you a spectacular view of the Amsterdam harbour as well. Perfect for some beautiful shots. You can access it via a pedestrian bridge. From the shore, REM Island makes for a cool picture itself.

FOOD AND DRINKS

BREAKFAST

Café de Pels

This local bar in the middle of de Negen Straatjes is a landmark. For over fifty years, it has been a reliable presence in an ever-changing urban landscape. This easy-going bar has a soul and a personality. From 9am, you can come in for a quick and tasty breakfast, consisting of boiled eggs, croissants, and jam.

Huidenstraat 25, 1016 ER (Centrum), cafedepels.nl

De Laatste Kruimel

This cosy little place in the heart of the city centre serves delicious scones, good coffee, and other freshly baked sweet treats. We also highly recommend their homemade quiches.

Langebrugsteeg 4, 1012 GB (Centrum), delaatstekruimel.com

Dignita Hoftuin

Certainly, one of the most beautiful breakfast spots in the city, hidden in an urban garden along the canal. In the glass-fronted restaurant, as well as on the sunny terrace behind the H'art Museum, dishes are presented like works of art: adorned with edible flowers and other delights.

Nieuwe Herengracht 18a, 1018 DP (Centrum), eatwelldogood.nl/dignita-hoftuin

Bakers & Roasters

What happens when a New Zealander and a Brazilian open a café in Amsterdam? You get a menu full of deliciousness at a fantastic location! The breakfast might be slightly pricier, but all products are environmentally conscious and focused on animal welfare. They also offer vegan options.

Kadijksplein 16, 1018 AC (Centrum), bakersandroasters.com

Café Restaurant Metro

This bar and restaurant boasts its own bakery, and that is apparent with every bite. You could easily hang about the whole day in this lovely open space.

Asterweg 22, 1031 HP (Noord), caferestaurantmetro.nl

The Breakfast Club

It's clear that the owners believe that the most important meal of the day is a good breakfast. And that isn't just true for mornings, as breakfast is served all day. On the menu, you'll find typical dishes from Mexico City, New York, and London. There are seven locations, so you will likely encounter one during your trip.

Wibautstraat 56, 1091 GN (Oost), thebreakfastclub.nl

Oeuf Amsterdam

Are you as big a fan of eggs as the owners Geza, Jeroen, and Tijn? Then Oeuf is the right place. With a shared passion for eggs, the three friends opened a breakfast/lunch spot with, no surprise there, dishes that revolve around eggs.

Daniël Stalpertstraat 36, 1072 BE (Zuid), oeufamsterdam.nl

De Wasserette

Just around the corner from Albert Cuyp Market, you'll find this all-day café on a nice little square. We're fans of the French toast and the Wasserette classic: bread with chicken, avocado, pancetta, truffle mayonnaise, and Parmigiano.

Eerste van der Helststraat 27, 1073 AC (Zuid), dewasserette.com

CT Coffee & Coconuts

A cinema in the 1920s, now a snug coffee and breakfast spot cherished by Amsterdammers. Enjoy a satisfying breakfast with one of the many fresh lemonades or freshly squeezed juices.

Ceintuurbaan 282, 1072 GK (Zuid), coffeeand-coconuts.com

SALVO Bake House

The unique Italian creations they make at SALVO could be classified as 'unreal.' The amounts of cream in the *maritozzi*, the croissants carbonara, all products with pistachio, and many other delicacies on rotation make it a culinary delight. Prepare for some unexpected flavours!

Tweede Hugo de Grootstraat 9, 1052 LA (West), salvobakehouse.com

Pacific Amsterdam

You can come here every day, all day: from breakfast to dinner. In the evening, they open the bar, and during weekends, the place transforms into a club. Bring a board game and settle down, or take a look at the art gallery.

Polonceaukade 23, 1014 DA (West), pacificam-sterdam.nl

COFFEE

Bocca Coffee

One of the most renowned cafés in town. It's a wonderfully tranquil spot in the bustling city centre, perfect for taking a moment to relax. They also offer brewing, tasting, and cocktail workshops.

Kerkstraat 96H, 1017 GP (Centrum), bocca.nl

White Label Coffee

A well-known coffee roastery based in Amsterdam, offering high-quality coffee to suit every taste. With several locations across the city, there's likely one near you. It's lovely to start the day with a cup of their White Label Coffee.

Zonneplein 4, 1033 EK (Noord), whitelabelcoffee.nl

Rum Baba Coffee Roasters

A comfortable coffee bar with its own coffee roastery, offering excellent filter coffee as well as tasty decaf options. You can buy their coffee by the bag to enjoy Amsterdam's finest at home.

Pretoriusstraat 15, 1092 EW (Oost), rumbaba.nl

Scandinavian Embassy

Next to Sarphatipark, you'll find this beautiful minimalist coffee bar in Scandi style. Apart from good coffee, you can also enjoy breakfast and lunch at Scandinavian Embassy.

Sarphatipark 34, 1072 PB (Zuid), scandinavianembassy.nl

Coffee Bru

A delightful coffee bar serving the tastiest cappuccinos. They offer some delicious banana bread too, if you're feeling peckish. Their Oost location also boasts a lovely terrace.

Van Woustraat 113, 1074 AH (Zuid), coffeebru.nl

Cafecito

Head to this modern and spacious espresso bar if you want a good cup of coffee without any fuss. The baristas know how to make delicious coffee and specialties like red velvet latte and matcha latte.

Van Baerlestraat 83, 1071 AS (Zuid), cafecito.nl

Stach

With nearly twenty locations in Amsterdam and even more throughout the Netherlands, Stach is an essential on this list. And delicious coffee is just the beginning, they offer a variety of other tasty products such as specialty sandwiches, chocolate, and ready-to-go (hot) meals.

Overtoom 112, 1054 HL (West), stach-food.nl

Zizou

Zizou, the owner's dog has stolen our hearts. And so has this lovely coffee spot in West named after it. It has everything you need: a relaxed place with great coffee with an incredibly friendly and genuine crowd.

Admiraal de Ruijterweg 4, 1056 GJ (West), insta @zizoucoffee

↓ DE WASSERETTE

↓ EETSALON VAN DOBBEN

KROKETTEN & UITSMIJTERS

Eetsalon Van Dobben

In a street off Rembrandtplein, standing strong since 1945, you'll find Eetsalon Van Dobben. Artists, football players, tourists, and locals have been coming here for decades. They're famous for their tasty *kroketten* (croquettes), but don't overlook their *ossenworst* roll (raw beef sausage) or *filet americain* either. A nostalgic place that we love.

Korte Reguliersdwarsstraat 5-7-9, 1017 BH (Centrum), eetsalonvandobben.nl

Café Kale

Another one of those iconic spots in the city where you can go for a good grilled cheese sandwich or (shrimp) croquettes roll, made by the equally iconic pastry shop Holtkamp. When the sun is out, their terrace offers a good spot to soak up some rays.

Weteringschans 267, 1017 XJ (Centrum), cafekale.nl

Café 't Hooischip

A small and welcoming bar by the river Amstel, near Waterlooplein. Go there for traditional Dutch lunch dishes such as *uitsmijter* (fried eggs with ham or cheese) or a roll with *rookworst* (smoked sausage), cheese, or meatballs.

Amstel 31, 1011 PT (Centrum), hooischip.nl

Café Gambrinus

A timeless bar and eatery in De Pijp, where you can enjoy drinks (lots of draft beers) with great snacks which never disappoint. Their terrace is in a nice spot as well.

Ferdinand Bolstraat 180, 1072 LV (Zuid), gambrinus.nl

LUNCH

Rue La Bastille

Authentic Mediterranean cuisine with a modern Algerian twist and good vibes. Choose one of the many fresh products from the colourful counter and create your own dish. Don't miss out on the delicious baklava: it's clear that a lot of love went into it.

Haarlemmerdijk 66H, 1013 JE (Centrum-West), ruelabastille.nl

CREA Café

Located next to the University of Amsterdam, this is a warm and welcoming place where local students like to gather. The people of CREA Café organise fun events such as lectures, expos, and workshops, while serving simple sandwiches, snacks, and soups at fair prices.

Nieuwe Achtergracht 170, 1018 WV (Centrum), crea.nl

Café de Ceuvel

You can find this cool place on a former shipyard, by the water, of course. It's frequented by local creatives. Enjoy one of the flavourful dishes from the fully plant-based menu. When it's sunny, you can take a dip in the channel.

Korte Papaverweg 4, 1032 KB (Noord), deceuvel.nl

Het Mandelahuisje

Hello, beautifully hidden spot surrounded by water! The summer terrace opens between May and September. But only when the weather is deemed good enough, which is a minimum of 17 degrees and preferably dry. Aunt Ivy is the resident chef, and her Surinamese *roti* is simply irresistible.

Sixhavenweg 27, 1021 HG (Noord), mandelahuisje.nl

Tolhuistuin

One of the cultural hotspots of the city, with many performances, and other artistic events. It's a beautiful place with a very stylish decor to have drinks, lunch, or dinner.

IJpromenade 2, 1031 KT (Noord), tolhuistuin.nl

Bar Botanique

We love this green oasis where the staff's tropical outfits match the interior. Go there for great breakfast, lunch, and dinner. The cocktails are top-notch too!

Eerste Van Swindenstraat 581, 1093 LC (Oost), barbotanique.nl

Gent aan de Schinkel

Oh, how we adore this place at the end of Vondelpark, with its bustling and lively terrace. A Belgian beer in hand, and something tasty from the extensive lunch menu on the table: Gent aan de Schinkel is always a good idea.

Theophile de Bockstraat 1, 1058 TV (Zuid), gentaandeschinkel.nl

BROODJES (ROLLS)

Gewoon Kaas

Nothing beats a good old *broodje kaas* (cheese roll), and this cheese shop and lunchroom offers plenty of choice from different types of delicious Dutch (and foreign) cheeses. Don't hesitate to ask for the staff's recommendation.

Middenweg 45, 1098 AC (Oost), gewoonkaas.nl

De Osdorper

A simple but fantastic place for delicious rolls. No fuss or trendy vibes, just good quality rolls and paninis.

Scheldestraat 32, 1078 GL (Zuid)

Toni's Deli

In this deli, you'll find irresistible *focaccias*. They might be a bit pricier, but given their size, you can easily share one.

Van Spilbergenstraat 2, 1057 RG (West), Insta @tonis.amsterdam

STREET FOOD

Lebanese Sajeria

Get yourself a delicious *manousheh*: flatbread filled with vegetables and other tasty Lebanese flavours. Then head to Amstelveld around the corner, take a seat at one of the benches and enjoy the laid-back vibe on this spacious square between canals.
Utrechtsestraat 69, 1017 VJ (Centrum), thesajeria.com

Kras Haring

It's by no means a stretch to say Nico and Annie serve the tastiest herring in Amsterdam, at their kiosk on a charming square opposite Het Scheepvaartmuseum. Herring is available year-round, but the fresh catch is in June.
Kattenburgerplein 89, 1018 KM (Centrum-Oost), krasharing.nl

Patisserie Holtkamp

Patisserie Holtkamp, in their classic and beautiful Art Deco building, is an Amsterdam icon. Founded by Cees and Petra, but now run by their daughter and son-in-law. You can go there for delicious savoury snacks, but please also treat yourself to one of their incredible sweet treats like syrup waffles, cheesecake, or chocolate cream puffs.
Vijzelgracht 15, 1017 HM (Centrum), patisserieholtkamp.nl

Zero Zero

Large in size as well as in flavour: you'll enjoy delicious sourdough *schiacciata* (an Italian sandwich), topped with high-quality Italian ingredients such as *mortadella*, *bresaola* and *gorgonzola dulce*.
Nieuwe Spiegelstraat 3A, 1017 DB (Centrum), zero-zero.store

FEBO

You're likely to come across the red-and-white letters of FEBO snack bar quite often in the city, as there are nearly thirty outlets in Amsterdam. The chain is named after Ferdinand Bolstraat. Get yourself a classic Dutch snack 'from the wall', and try a *frikandel*, *kroket*, or *kaas-soufflé*. It's part of the culture. FEBO Buikslotermeerplein was the last to win *Best FEBO Of The Year*.

Buikslotermeerplein 54 1025 EW (Noord), febo.nl

Tigris & Eufraat

This friendly supermarket and delicatessen has been a go-to spot in bustling Javastraat for years. Taste the flavours of the Middle East in their popular falafel in Syrian flatbread. The shawarma also comes highly recommended.

Javastraat 20H, 1094 HH (Oost), insta @ tigriseneufraat_official

Venetië IJs

One of the best ice cream parlours in the city, old-fashioned and charming with genuine Italian flavours. Only open during the summer months.

Scheldestraat 68, 1078 GM (Zuid)

Warung Barokah

Warung is Indonesian for eatery, and Warung Barokah is one of the best there is. Traditional Indonesian classics such as *soto soup*, *goreng rames*, and *gado gado* are featured on the menu.

Aalsmeerweg 91, 1059 AE (Zuid), warung-barokah.nl

Bir Tat

A favourite among connoisseurs. Freshly grilled Turkish dishes, do we need to say more? Don't forget to try one of the sweet snacks as well, *kunefe* is our favourite.

Bos en Lommerweg 242, 1055 EJ (West), birtat.nl

Dumplings

A hidden, plain kiosk next to Westerpark, offering super fresh, authentic dumplings and other tasty Chinese delicacies.
Nassauplein 60, 1052 AH (West)

Neighbourhood markets

We love the bustling markets of Amsterdam; each neighbourhood has its own. Ten Katemarkt in Kinkerbuurt is definitely a winner. An abundance of stalls and international cuisines, you'll always find something delicious. Another favourite is Dappermarkt in Oost: a vibrant market, where you can find clothes and cosmetics as well as lots of delicious foods. Try Best Döner at the corner of the market, very well-known in the area.
Ten Katestraat, 1053 CG (West) and Dapperstraat, 1093 BS (Oost)

BEER & BITTERBALLEN

The name for the Dutch meat-based fried snack *bitterballen* is associated with *bitter*, alcoholic drinks flavoured with herbs, fruit, or spices. Nowadays, the breadcrumb covered balls made from a thick meaty stew, will usually be devoured alongside a beer rather than a bitter.

Café 't Gasthuys

A great place to grab a quick bite, serving classic dishes like spareribs, satay, and Dutch snacks including *bitterballen*, and cheese. Affordable above all and a friendly atmosphere.
Grimburgwal 7, 1012 GA (Centrum), gasthuys.nl

Café De Druif

One of the oldest bars in town, and it's always buzzing at De Druif. The building dates back to the 16th century, and you can really feel the history, with its old-school interior and the vintage photos hanging on the walls. They serve a wide range of drinks, so take your pick.

Rapenburgerplein 83, 1011 VJ (Centrum), cafededruif.nl

Brouwerij 't IJ

It doesn't get more Dutch than this: enjoying a freshly brewed cold beer, *bitterballen*, and some cheese dipped in mustard whilst sitting under a windmill. You can soak up the sun on their large terrace. English spoken brewery tours are available for a small contribution on Fridays, Saturdays, and Sundays at 3.30pm.

Funenkade 7, 1018 AL (Oost), brouwerijhetij.nl

DINNER

Thai Snackbar Bird

Generally, dining on Zeedijk means quality and authenticity. You can find many Asian establishments here, one of which is Snackbar Bird (don't confuse it with the restaurant opposite). It's cramped and noisy inside, but the food is oh so delicious. With delightful curries, fish cakes, satay, and dozens of other typical Thai dishes on the menu. The daily special is takeout only. Fancy a drink after dinner? Café Fonteyn at the Nieuwmarkt is always a good idea, it's only a 5 minute walk away.

Zeedijk 77, 1012 AS (Centrum), thaibird.nl

Hanneke's boom

In a city surrounded by water, you must try this unique and colourful spot by the canal. You'll sit at picnic tables on the large terrace while enjoying a nice, cool drink. If your wallet allows, you'll find some tasty food to feast on.

Dijksgracht 4, 1019 BS (Centrum), hannekesboom.nl

Waterkant Amsterdam

An established Amsterdam spot where a lively atmosphere is guaranteed, as well as good company, delicious Surinamese-inspired food, and great drinks. Perfect for shared dining. On Fridays and Saturdays, you can stay until 3am for its subsequent club night. This might be the best terrace of the city.

Marnixstraat 246, 1016 TL (Centrum), waterkantamsterdam.nl

Taste of Culture

If you're travelling in a group, this Chinese restaurant is perfect to dine in. Ask for the round table when booking, and order plenty of the authentic dishes to share. Don't miss out on the Peking duck. You won't regret ordering it!

Korte Leidsedwarsstraat 139-141, 1017 PZ (Centrum), tasteofcultureamsterdam.nl

Eetcafé Skek

This cultural no-nonsense café is run by students. With a changing menu featuring seasonal products, local beers, fair prices, and always plenty of conviviality. Check their calendar for their activities, including music, poetry, and pub quizzes.

Zeedijk 4-8, 1012 AX (Centrum), skekamsterdam.nl

Umaimon

In Japanese ramen, good broth is essential, and at Umaimon you can choose between different types. They are all equally delicious, but the creamy chicken broth is our secret winner. Their toppings range from classic pork and fried or teriyaki chicken to a number of vegan options, which are just as flavourful as the classics. A large bowl of ramen should do, but if you're very hungry or can't resist temptation, be sure to try the gyoza and the (spicy) takoyaki as well.

Korte Leidsedwarsstraat 51, 1017 PW (Centrum), takumiramennoodles.com

Café Kadijk

Go to this snug restaurant for traditional and delicious Indonesian dishes such as satay and *rendang*. With a lovely terrace.

Kadijksplein, 1018 AB (Centrum), cafekadijk.nl

Pazzi

Pizza fans beware: Pazzi serves wood-fired pizzas that are still made according to traditional recipes. They are just too tasty! They also serve a wide range of *antipasti*. A taste of Italy in the middle of Amsterdam. Fully booked? Don't worry, there are five other locations dotted throughout the city.

Eerste Looiersdwarsstraat 4, 1016 VM (Centrum), pazziamsterdam.nl

Xi'an Delicious Foods

Xi'an is a Chinese city, as well as a great eatery in Amsterdam, Rotterdam, and The Hague. They serve delicious hand-pulled noodles. The Chinese crêpes are another reason we keep coming back.

Lange Leidsedwarsstraat 21H, 1017 NE (Centrum), xianfoods.nl

Pllek

From this lovely spot by the water, you overlook the Amsterdam skyline, primarily enjoying vegetarian and vegan dishes. They serve some surprising dishes and flavours. Some meat and fish are on offer, all sourced as sustainably as possible. We're big fans, especially when the sun's out and we can chill on the spacious terrace.

T.T. Neveritaweg 59, 1033 WB (Noord), pllek.nl

La Fucina

This is such a lovely place, you'd prefer to keep it all to yourself. In a street with so much deliciousness to be found, sometimes you don't know where to begin. But La Fucina is always a good idea, with their delicious paninis and rectangular pizzas loaded with flavourful toppings.

Javastraat 99, 1094 HC (Oost), lafucina.nl

Eddy Spaghetti

Come to Eddy for Italian classics like *pasta carbonara, arrabbiata, affogato,* and *tiramisu.* And for the great atmosphere. Staff is attentive and friendly, and the dishes are just as they should be.

Krugerplein 23, 1092 KA (Oost), eddyspaghetti.nl

Café De Jeugd

'Growing old can wait' is the motto of De Jeugd ('The Youth'), a bar with a vintage interior. With its tasty snacks, burgers, cocktails, karaoke nights, board games, and cheerful atmosphere, your dinner seamlessly transitions into even more fun.

Linnaeusstraat 37A, 1093 EG (Oost), deeeuwigejeugd.nl

Peperwortel

In a fantastically beautiful location next to Vondelpark, nestled among the wild foliage, you'll find this homely little restaurant. You can order single slices of quiche, well-filled pitas, and other tasty snacks.

Overtoom 140, 1054 HN (West), peperwortel.nl

Fenan Klein Afrika

Have you ever tried Ethiopian cuisine? In this atmospheric and relaxed restaurant, you can enjoy delicious spices, with great meat dishes involving lamb and chicken, as well as flavourful vegetarian options with surprising ingredients. And use your hands! Shared dining as it should be.

Jan Pieter Heijestraat 147, 1054 MG (West), fenankleinafrika-amsterdam.nl

Rotisserie & Van 't Spit

All your guilty pleasures come together in De Clercqstraat: tender chicken, excellent fries, burgers, homemade apple sauce. It doesn't get much better than this. Two rotisseries spots that are practically neighbours.

De Clercqstraat 81H & 95, 1053 AG (West), rotisserieamsterdam.nl, vantspit.nl

BRING THE PARENTS

Toscanini

In this classic Italian restaurant with open kitchen on the beautiful Lindengracht, you'll be indulged in every way. The staff will deliver an unforgettable evening with high-quality Italian dishes.

Lindengracht 75, 1015 KD, (Centrum), restauranttoscanini.nl

Restaurant De Kas

A unique restaurant, hidden in a park, set up in a greenhouse where their own vegetables are grown. Food doesn't get any fresher than this. A beautiful spot with delicious wines to accompany each dish.

Kamerlingh Onneslaan 3, 1097 DE (Oost), restaurantdekas.com

↓ DE CEUVEL

GOING OUT

BARS

De Gieter

Café de Gieter, a longstanding favourite with the young crowd, sits at the heart of Leidseplein. With its chilled-out ambiance and fair prices it remains a cherished student hub.
Korte Leidsedwarsstraat 179, 1017 RA (Centrum)

Café Brecht

Step into this East German-inspired bar and embrace its living room atmosphere, complete with vintage decor and charming wallpaper. Informal and authentic. Enjoy their excellent draught beers, including some German favourites.
Weteringschans 157, 1017 SE (Centrum), insta @cafebrecht

Kopstootbar

Named after the traditional Dutch drink *kopstoot* (Dutch gin paired with beer), this bar is always ready to party. It's a great spot to start your evening, but leaving can be challenging once you're into the groove. It can get quite crowded.
Marnixstraat 429, 1017 PK (Centrum), kopstootbar.amsterdam

Café Weber

A bar as good as they come: classic ambiance and interior,

and good music to kick off your evening. Only a short walk from the bustling Leidseplein.

Marnixstraat 397, 1017 PJ (Centrum), barweber.nl

Wijnand Fockink Proeflokaal

No matter how busy it gets in this welcoming liquor store and distillery, the knowledgeable staff always take their time to ensure your drink is just the way you like it. With a nice mixture of tourists and locals who come here to end their working day. Try to sound like a local by ordering a *pikketanussie*, slang for a glass of Dutch gin (*jenever*).

Pijlsteeg 31, 1012 HH (Centrum), wynand-fockink.nl

De Prael

Brewery De Prael offers a wide array of home-brewed beers at two locations, in Centrum and in Zuid. We love De Prael for their commitment to inclusivity, offering opportunities to people with a labour market disadvantage, including those with visible or invisible disabilities.

Oudezijds Armsteeg 26, 1012 GP (Centrum), deprael.nl

Old Sailor

This typical Amsterdam bar, bang in the middle of the Red-Light District, is a perfect spot to watch the world go by. The nautical interior and the affordable drinks always attract a diverse crowd.

Oudezijds Achterburgwal 38a, 1012 DA (Centrum), cafeoldsailor.eu

Café Nol

It feels like you're stepping back in time. This typical old-fashioned Dutch *kroeg*, with a music choice to match, is a perfect setting for brushing up your Dutch language skills. A fun time is guaranteed.

Westerstraat 109, 1015 LX (Centrum), cafenol.amsterdam

Pilsvogel

This atmospheric bar, on a lively square in De Pijp, has been a local institution for years. The welcoming staff ensures a fun afternoon or evening. The tasty tapas are perfect for sharing.

Gerard Douplein 14, 1072 VE (Zuid), pilsvogel.nl

Bar Mimi

This local bistro offers a surprising menu, and they attract a very mixed crowd. Start your evening at Bar Mimi with some shared dishes and stay for some of their excellent drinks.

Potgieterstraat 35, 1053 XR (West), insta @ mimiamsterdam

COCKTAILS

Vesper

In the heart of the city, this classy cocktail bar offers a relaxed atmosphere with expertly crafted cocktails. With its intimate setting and regularly changing menu, it's a must-visit. They also offer workshops.
Vinkenstraat 57, 1013 JM (Centrum), vesperbar.nl

A'DAM Toren: MA'DAM & The Loft

On the top floor of the iconic A'DAM Tower, you'll find MA'DAM, a cool sky bar serving exceptionally good cocktails. With its stunning views, it's hard to beat. On the 16th floor, The Loft occasionally hosts club nights. Spectacular!
Overhoeksplein 1, 1031 KS (Noord), adamtoren.nl

Bar Bukowski

This bar serves up killer cocktails. With its hip décor and relaxed atmosphere, it is the perfect place to have a few drinks and a good time. The terrace is very inviting.
Oosterpark 10, 1092 AE (Oost), barbukowksi.nl

Calle Ocho

Calle Ocho offers a Latin American setting with its colourful décor, lively atmosphere and tasty street food like *tostadas* and *ceviche*. Savour delicious cocktails or choose from one of the many types of rum, tequila, and mezcal. Super friendly vibes and lots of fun.
Albert Cuypstraat 226, 1073 BN (Zuid), insta @calleochoams

Hachi

Whether you opt for a classic cocktail or want to experiment with new flavours, Hachi ensures a great time with its lovely bar staff and trendy decor. Always a very good ambiance.

Albert Cuypstraat 18, 1072 CT (Zuid), insta @ hachi_ams

QUEER

Club NYX

A vibrant nightlife spot, known for its diverse crowd and eclectic music. With multiple floors and themed parties, Club NYX is a hotspot for dancing and unforgettable experiences.

Reguliersdwarsstraat 42, 1017 BM (Centrum), clubnyx.nl

Club Church

Club Church is a safe and lively club known for its diverse and inclusive atmosphere, where all different sub-groups in the community feel welcomed. It offers various theme nights, performances, and parties.

Kerkstraat 52, 1017 GM (Centrum), clubchurch.nl

Lellebel

A fun bar known for its friendly atmosphere and diverse entertainment. Lellebel hosts karaoke nights, drag shows, and comedy events, creating a lively environment for its visitors.

Utrechtsestraat 4H, 1017 VN (Centrum), lellebel.nl

De Trut

This welcoming bar/club is an iconic spot in the city where volunteers run the show, the atmosphere is always great, and you'll feel safe due to De Trut's no-phone policy. Even more fun, right?

Bilderdijkstraat 165-E, 1053 KP (West), trutfonds.nl

PAMELA

A neighbourhood bar in West. Offers a relaxed atmosphere, perfect for unwinding with friends over drinks and some good conversation.

Jacob van Lennepstraat 86H, 1053 HM (West), insta @pamela.amsterdam

CLUBS

Melkweg

A renowned cultural venue hosting a wide range of concerts, club nights, and other events. With its diverse programming, Melkweg attracts both local and international audiences.
Lijnbaansgracht 234A, 1017 PH (Centrum), melkweg.nl

Bitterzoet

From Afro to hip-hop, and from folk rock to R&B, Bitterzoet offers exciting club nights and live performances catering to all sorts of musical preferences. The intimate atmosphere is perfect for both dancing and socialising.
Spuistraat 2 HS, 1012 TS (Centrum), bitterzoet.com

Chin Chin Club

This vibrant venue blurs the boundaries between dining and clubbing. With its bold décor, innovative cocktails, and eclectic menu inspired by Asian street food, Chin Chin Club promises an unforgettable culinary and social adventure.
Rozengracht 133, 1016 LV (Centrum), insta @chinchinclubams

Paradiso

Paradiso, legendary Temple of Pop, is a renowned venue for live music and cultural events. The former church offers a one-of-a-kind atmosphere. It hosts iconic performances while also nurturing emerging talents: David Bowie, Amy Winehouse, and Pink Floyd have all graced Paradiso's stage.
Weteringschans 6-8, 1017 SG (Centrum), paradiso.nl

Chicago Social Club

A cool club with two floors where house, techno, and hip-hop set the tone. It's a great place to enjoy energetic music and dance the night away.

Leidseplein 12, 1017 PT (Centrum), insta @ chicagosocialclub

Garage Noord

Former car repair shop turned underground club. Known for its gritty atmosphere and diverse music line-up, appealing to electronic music enthusiasts and local artists alike. We love the vibe in here!

Gedempt Hamerkanaal 40, 1021 KM (Noord), garagenoord.com

Skatecafé Karin & Yvonne

A vibrant hangout blending skating culture and café vibes. Go here for the laid-back atmosphere, the tasty bites, and the occasional live music event. A fun-filled evening is awaiting you.

Gedempt Hamerkanaal 42, 1021 KM (Noord), skatecafe.nl

Doka

Club Doka, nestled in the basement of Volkshotel in Oost, offers intimate vibes and eclectic DJ sets. It attracts a diverse crowd. On the rooftop, you'll find Canvas, a bar/restaurant with a cool terrace offering panoramic views. It's the perfect spot to unwind and take in the skyline.

Wibautstraat 150, 1091 GR (Oost), volkshotel. nl/doka

RADION

Club Radion is a dynamic venue for electronic music and underground parties. With its industrial surroundings and innovative DJ sets, it's a must-visit. Radion's café is open for dinner and drinks, Tuesdays to Fridays.

Louwesweg 1, 1066 EA (West), insta @ radionamsterdam

Tilla Tec

For years, club De School was a leading venue in the dance scene. Its successor Tilla Tec Club serves as a cultural hub hosting club nights, exhibitions, and other cultural events.

Jan van Breemenstraat 1, 1056AB (West), insta @tillatec

Lofi

Situated in an industrial warehouse, club Lofi exudes an underground atmosphere. Its intimate electronic music events and DJ sets across diverse genres offer a raw and immersive experience.

Basisweg 63, 1043 AN (West), lofi. amsterdam

↓ KING'S DAY

HOW TO DRESS LIKE A LOCAL

As is often the case in the world of fashion, Amsterdam residents are sensitive to trends. They like to be trendsetters as well. Once a trend has been set, it cannot be unseen. There are a few constant factors: comfort and practicality are key. No high heels to go clubbing; deemed impractical, and trainers are much more comfortable anyway. Opt for relaxed fits and versatile pieces that you can easily wear from day to night.

Then there's that 'natural' look: pretending you've just grabbed something from the closet with your eyes closed, while the full outfit is carefully styled. Local brands are a common denominator, Amsterdammers take pride in their local designers and shops. Think of brands like Bonne Suits, Lack of Guidance, and Patta.

Just like any other city, Amsterdam has its subcultures. People often connect their identity to their neighbourhood, the bars they frequent, the friends they have, and the university they attend; and therefore, the clothes and brands they wear. Firstly, there's the normcore group wearing Adidas Gazelles and wide-leg trousers. Then there's gorpcore, wearing Patagonia jumpers and hiking boots. For the urban look, quiet luxury is the norm: expensive clothes without prominently visible branding. The nouveau-riche on the other hand, like their luxury to be very visible and a status symbol.

These are just a few examples; people experiment and try to be different. How to dress like a local? Embrace individuality: Amsterdam's fashion scene is all about expressing your unique style. Don't be afraid to mix and match different pieces to create your own look.

FLEA MARKETS, VINTAGE & SECOND-HAND

Waterlooplein

Waterlooplein, 1011 PG (Centrum-Oost), waterlooplein.amsterdam

Waterlooplein, situated in the heart of Amsterdam, hosts a bustling daily market brimming with eclectic gems. The vibrant hub offers everything from vintage clothes and antiques to quirky souvenirs, and fresh produce. Bargain hunters and culture enthusiasts alike flock to its stalls, creating a lively atmosphere against the backdrop of historical landmarks. From Dutch delicacies to global flavours, food vendors tantalise taste buds while street performers entertain passers-by. The Waterlooplein market isn't just a shopping destination; it's a cultural melting pot where the essence of Amsterdam's diverse spirit comes alive.

Noordermarkt

Noordermarkt 48, 1015 NA (Centrum), noordermarkt-amsterdam.nl

One of Amsterdam's oldest and now most popular markets is located at the foot of Noorderkerk. This local market is open Monday mornings and all day on Saturdays. You'll find plenty of organic treats, second-hand pieces, old books, and antique furniture. Just around the corner, on Westerstraat, you'll find Patch Market, with all sorts of clothes, bags, and accessories.

CARDS
1= €1.50
4= €5
Girl
AMSTERDAM
WITH LOVE
HOLLAND
HOLLAND
HOLLAND

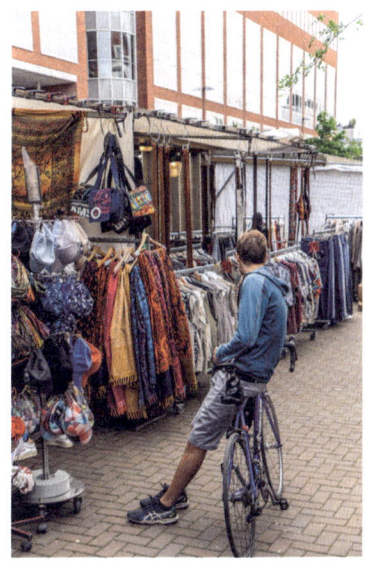

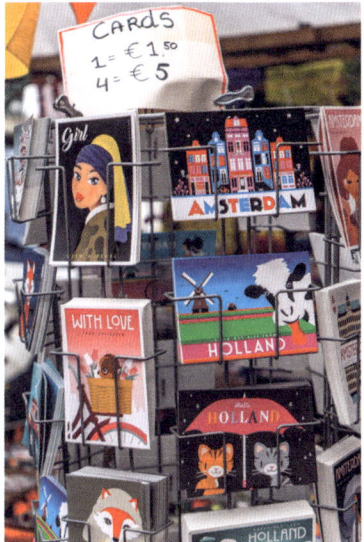

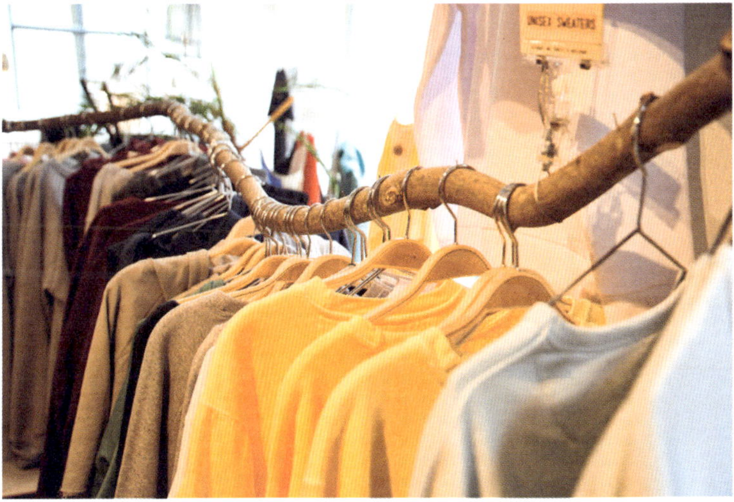

Zipper Vintage Clothing

Huidenstraat 7,
1016 ER (Centrum),
zippervintageclothing.com

In one of the charming Nine Streets, Huidenstraat, you'll discover this shop with its living room ambiance. Here, you'll find second-hand and vintage clothes from the 1950s to the present. The stock is replenished weekly, with some amazing items to be discovered. Zipper also restyles brought-in second-hand clothes to turn them into even more special pieces.

Jutka & Riska

Haarlemmerdijk 143,
1013 KG (Centrum),
Bilderdijkstraat 194, 1053
LE (West), jutkaenriska.
com

Fashion-forward sisters Jutka and Riska own four shops, two of which in Amsterdam. Alongside vintage finds, you'll also discover their own designs, sunglasses, and bags. Always original, daring, and full of character. They also have a shop in Haarlem, which could make for a fun daytrip out of Amsterdam (see page 182).

Vijzel Vintage

Vijzelstraat 83,
1017 HG (Centrum)
Bilderdijkstraat 194,
1053 LE (West),
jutkaenriska.com

Love it or hate it, opinions about and experiences with the shop owner may vary, but if you're a vintage lover, you'll definitely find excellent pieces at Vijzel Vintage. The owner offers his (unsolicited) advice, and if you can handle it, it can be a fantastic shopping experience. A shop with a personality.

Marbles Vintage

Haarlemmerdijk 64,
1013JE (Centrum),
Staalstraat 30, 1011 JM
(Centrum),
Ferdinand Bolstraat 28,
1072LK (Zuid),
Insta @marblesvintage

A treasure trove for vintage. Located in the heart of Amsterdam, this boutique offers a curated selection of unique clothes and accessories from past decades. From funky 70s prints to timeless 90s grunge, there's something for every style and preference. The store's eclectic atmosphere makes browsing a delight. Whether you're hunting for a statement piece or simply browsing, Marbles Vintage promises a nostalgic journey through fashion history.

Lena The Fashion Library

Westerstraat 174,
1015 MP (Centrum),
lena-library.com

We're super excited to share this concept with you: at Lena, you can buy beautiful items or rent them. It's more sustainable and helps to prevent impulse buys. You can even rent an item for just an evening to make a statement at the club, for example. You simply return it the next day. We absolutely love this initiative!

Mokum Vintage

Rozengracht 25, 1016 LR
(Centrum-West), insta @
mokum_vintage

Mokum Vintage is a beloved second-hand clothes shop, named after the city's nickname. It offers an extensive selection of used streetwear and designer brands. With regular new arrivals, there's always something new to discover. It's good value for money as well.

Laura Dols

Wolvenstraat 7, 1016 EM
(Centrum), lauradols.nl

The ultimate destination for lovers of vintage dresses and accessories. Located in a charming building in the historic centre, this colourful boutique offers an extensive collection of beautiful dresses from various eras, ranging from glamorous 1920s flapper style to elegant 1950s silhouettes. You'll also find matching accessories such as hats and gloves. With expert advice and a nostalgic atmosphere, Laura Dols is a must-visit for enthusiasts of timeless fashion and vintage elegance.

Bij Ons Vintage

Nieuwezijds Voorburgwal
150, 1012 SJ (Centrum),
bijonsvintage.com

You can find any piece of clothing here, but the focus is mainly on the 70s and 80s. In addition to clothes, you can also find vintage accessories, and even some furniture at Bij Ons. If you haven't been able to find that one vintage gem, you'll get another chance in their second shop. Every week, a new supply of vintage items comes in.

IJ-hallen

T.T. Neveritaweg 15, 2012
ZM (Noord), ijhallen.nl

The IJ-hallen are renowned within and beyond the city, as they host Europe's largest, most charming flea market. Each month, for one weekend, hundreds of vendors display an array of beautiful products. Expect not just clothes but household items as well; you can find just about anything here. Arrive early if want to take a unique keepsake home; the best finds tend to go quickly. Whether you're a seasoned collector or simply enjoy browsing, the IJ-hallen promise a delightful shopping experience amidst a lively entourage. You'll need a ticket to enter.

Garment

*Molukkenstraat 23g, 1095
AR (Oost), garment.nl*

This pre-loved clothes shop, tucked away in Oost, is a gem cherished by locals. Curated by the discerning eye of owner Natascha, each piece reflects her impeccable taste. Alongside these pre-loved gems, the shop features new items from ethical and sustainable brands. This is more than just shopping; it's a community-driven haven where style meets sustainability and conviviality reigns supreme. Enhance your shopping experience with a visit to the charming neighbourhood café BAR JOOST, just a few doors down.

We Are Vintage

*Eerste Van Swindenstraat
43, 1093 GC (Oost),
Kinkerstraat 193, 1053 DR
(West), rumorsvintage.nl*

Trying to find affordable and unique pieces? Look no further! Explore various fashion styles from the 70s to the 90s and let your creativity run wild. From bags to shoes, and from scarves to cool jackets, you'll surely find something that catches your eye. Whether you're into retro vibes or searching for a statement piece, this shop has got you covered. Dive in and uncover fashion delights from decades past.

Kringloopwinkel Kerk & Buurt

*De Wittenkade 111, 1052
AG (West)ZM (Noord),
ijhallen.nl*

Away from the trendy shopping streets and bustling crowds, you'll find Kerk & Buurt. It's a second-hand shop in a church basement, offering items like vinyl records, household goods, and a selection of second-hand clothes. The proceeds support charitable projects run by Kerk & Buurt.

Vintage Jungle

Witte de Withstraat 114, 1057 ZG (West), vintagejungle.nl

The two sisters who run this shop, Marlot and Imara, grew up surrounded by flea markets and vintage clothes. With real collectors as parents, their passion for vintage and second-hand items started early. They therefore consider it important that all the items they sell are selected with love and care. You'll find vintage clothes from all over the world at Vintage Jungle.

STREETWEAR

Maha Amsterdam

*Vijzelstraat 129,
1017 HJ (Centrum),
nl.maha-amsterdam.com*

Maha, founded in 2015, aims to represent women in the Amsterdam streetwear market. The shop offers a range of trendy fashion and the latest trainers. A fun fact: even the Amsterdam mayor is a fan and enjoys shopping there! With a focus on empowerment and style, Maha has established itself as a hotspot for fashion-conscious women seeking unique and contemporary pieces.

Bonne Suits

*Warmoesstraat 67, 1012
HX (Centrum), insta @
bonnesuits*

This shop/gallery is more than just a nice place that sells handmade unisex suits. Founder Bonne Reijn creates a relaxed space for creatives in his shop, with regular exhibitions, and the possibility to make music.

Patta

Zeedijk 68-70, 1012 BA (Centrum), patta.nl

This brand, named for the Surinamese word for trainer, was founded in 2009. It is renowned for its streetwear and collaborations with other cool brands. They blend urban vibes with quality, ensuring their gear is not only stylish but also comfortable. Patta is streetwise and coveted by fashion enthusiasts globally, making it a must-have for those who love the street-style scene. Their flagship store is located on buzzing Zeedijk.

Daily Paper

Bilderdijkstraat 131, 1053 KN (West), dailypaperclothing.com

Daily Paper is a hip streetwear brand with roots in Africa. Renowned for its bold designs inspired by the continent's cultural diversity, the brand embraces striking prints and high-quality materials. Daily Paper offers a unique style that resonates with the global street-fashion scene, quickly gaining popularity and becoming a favourite among youths worldwide.

Olaf Hussein

Bilderdijkstraat 112, 1053 KZ (West), olafhussein. comdaily

Olaf Hussein, a cool clothing brand, brings a blend of minimalist style and timeless elegance. Founded by designer Olaf Hussein himself, the brand is recognised for its high-quality materials and sleek designs that effortlessly merge casual and chic. The collections reflect a modern, urban vibe, making the shop a must-visit for those seeking effortless style, and quality.

DEPARTMENT STORES

HEMA

Kalverstraat 212, 1012 XH (Centrum), hema.nl

Discover the vibrant energy of HEMA on Kalverstraat, where trendy design and affordability converge. The perfect place for young people (okay, adults too ...) to find everything from cool school supplies to fashionable accessories. With its lively atmosphere and versatile range, HEMA is a shopping experience that suits a youthful style. Don't miss out on their famous *broodje rookworst*, a bun filled with their signature smoked sausage.

De Bijenkorf

Dam 1, 1012 JS (Centrum), debijenkorf.nl

Slap bang in the middle of Amsterdam, you'll find the most famous department store of the Netherlands, to gasp at luxury brands like Gucci, Louis Vuitton, and Valentino. There are some more affordable brands on offer too, but it is mainly a high-end affair.

Magna Plaza

Nieuwezijds Voorburgwal 182I, 1012 SJ (Centrum), magnaplaza.nl

Located a stone's throw from Dam Square, this historic shopping centre is housed in a former post office dating back to 1899. The neo renaissance building hosts luxury shops and dining establishments. With its glass dome, it provides a beautiful shopping experience and stunning views of the city.
This upscale shopping centre in Amsterdam-

Gelderlandplein

Van Leijenberghlaan 43, 1082 GC (Zuid), gelderlandplein.nl

Zuid offers an elegant shopping experience with a mix of boutiques, well-known brands, and gourmet delights. Surrounded by greenery and modern architecture, it's a charming destination. With boutiques, bookshops, and trendy cafes, it provides a vibrant atmosphere.

↓ DE BIJENKORF

BOOKSHOPS

**Athenaeum
Boekhandel**

*Spui 14-16, 1012 XA
(Centrum), athenaeum.nl*

Athenaeum Boekhandel's flagship store on the small, convivial Spui square, has been a most welcome sight to the people of Amsterdam since 1966. Here, you'll find not only an extensive selection of Dutch, English, German, French, and Spanish literature and non-fiction, but also a great range of (international) magazines. In case you're always on the lookout for new recommendations: their newsletters are based on your preferences and curated by one of their knowledgeable booksellers.

Scheltema

*Rokin 9, 1012 KK
(Centrum), scheltema.nl*

Scheltema (pronunciation might be a tad difficult!) is only one minute away from Dam square, making it a perfect bookish hideaway from this particularly busy part of the city. With its four floors, it's one of the largest bookshops in Amsterdam, making it all the more difficult not to spend your entire budget in there. On the third floor, you'll find an entire section focused on travel guides, maps, atlases, and travel literature. Need a break after browsing? Take a seat at the in-house café Vascobelo for breakfast, lunch, or a sweet treat.

Waterstones

Kalverstraat 152,
1012 XE (Centrum),
waterstones.com

Did you know that British chain Waterstones has a branch in Amsterdam? Now you do! This haven for book lovers is located in a monumental building in Kalverstraat, one of the city's most important (and busiest) shopping streets. Their assortment not only consists of (English) fiction and nonfiction, but also stationary, board games, bookmarks, and other bookish items. Special and limited editions usually only found across the pond are also stocked here. Note that the three upper levels are accessible only via staircases.

The American Book Center

Spui 12, 1012 XA (Centrum), abc.nl

It's all in the name. At The American Book Center – also called The ABC – you'll find a large number of English-language books. Not all American, they also stock U.K. editions. Definitely stop by if you're a fan of graphic novels, manga, and comics. Don't forget to pay a visit to Betty the Book Machine on the second floor – she's regularly printing, binding, and trimming self-published books.

The Book Exchange

Kloveniersburgwal 58, 1012 CX (Centrum), bookexchange.nl

This bookshop is like a maze; even when you think you have reached the end, there always seems to be another room chock full of second-hand books. At The Book Exchange, you'll find a great range of books about photography, architecture, history, and society, but also a large section of young adult, fiction, and nonfiction books. Some shelves are beyond reach – we weren't exaggerating when we said 'chock full' – so if you can't find the book you're looking for on the main shelves, ask the owner for help.

Oudemanhuispoort book market

Oudemanhuispoort, 1012 CN (Centrum)

Near The Book Exchange, between Oudezijds Achterburgwal and Kloveniersburgwal, you can find Oudemanhuispoort book market. In this alleyway, located near the faculty of Humanities and Philosophy of the University of Amsterdam, you'll find a few stalls with second-hand books of all sorts and sizes. Some of the stalls have a 'proper' little shop as well, complete with a ladder to get to the top shelves. You can delve into your 'new' book in the nearby courtyard, a secret local spot hidden in plain sight.

Happy Boekieman

Herengracht 267A,
1016 BJ (Centrum),
fb @HappyBoekieman

This little second-hand bookshop is hidden at Herengracht. The shop is based in the living room of its owner, who is always ready for a chat. You can come in 24/7 and take a copy for just € 1.50!

Linnaeus Boekhandel

Middenweg 29,
1098 AB (Oost),
linnaeusboekhandel.nl

What makes Linnaeus Boekhandel worth a visit is not only their extensive assortment of books in all genres, but also the incredibly knowledgeable staff. Whether you're looking for a specific title or a personal recommendation, their booksellers are always prepared to help. They stock a large section. You can take your new book(s) to the nearby Oosterpark, sit down, and read for a bit before moving on.

Minibiebs

When you're out and about, keep your eyes peeled for the so-called *minibiebs* (mini libraries) They can be found all over Amsterdam, usually in residential areas, and take on various forms. The rules are pretty simple: if you see a book you like, you can take it with you – there's no need to return it. If you happen to have a book with you that you don't mind leaving behind, it would be appreciated if you did, so the minibieb is well-stocked for the next person to find it. To find a minibieb near you, have a look at the map made by Emile and Enkiri of the Instagram page @ *minibiebsofamsterdam*.

ART SUPPLIES

De Posthumus Winkel

Sint Luciënsteeg 25,
1012 PM (Centrum),
posthumuswinkel.nl

Upgrade your letters, postcards and (travel) journals with stamps from De Posthumus Winkel. This specialty shop has hundreds of them on offer, in varying themes such as the beach and sea, animals, flowers, letters, and even full sentences. You'll also find plain writing paper and envelopes, which you can decorate with your newly bought stamps. Book lovers who pride themselves in their personal libraries will enjoy their ex libris collection.

Vlieger

Amstel 34, 1017 AB (Centrum), vliegerpapier.nl

Don't be fooled by the unassuming and narrow façade of Vlieger. Once inside, you'll see that the shop is much bigger than you'd initially thought, and much more colourful as well. Stacks and stacks of paper, in all shades, shapes and sizes, as well as notebooks, sketchbooks, Japanese envelopes, and quality paints line the walls of this historical building. Always wanted to try your hand at bookbinding? You'll find everything you need.

Koud Kunstje

Rozengracht 49E, 1016 LR (Centrum), koudkunstje.nl

Does your craft box need to be replenished? Go to Koud Kunstje, a cute craft shop in the heart of Amsterdam. Named for the Dutch variant of the phrase 'a piece of cake', which incorporates the word for art. Everything related to crafting, from Fimo clay to foam rubber ... you name it, Koud Kunstje has it. Owner Maartje is always ready to give you crafting advice.

P.W. Akkerman

Langebrugsteeg 13, 1012 GB (Centrum), pwakkerman.com

When they think of fountain pens, Amsterdammers think of P.W. Akkerman. You can choose your own colourful, unique, or luxurious pen, adding a bit of joy to work or study. The pens in this shop aren't throwaway by any means, so you might have to save up a little before shopping at P.W. Akkerman.

AFFORDABLE ART AND HOME DECO

Art Amsterdam Spui

Spui 20HS, 1012 XA (Centrum), artamsterdam-spui.com

Every Sunday from March to December, an art market takes place on Spui. A great place to buy the most beautiful souvenir or Amsterdam keepsake. Affordable paintings, ceramics, jewellery, and drawings are on offer, made mostly by Dutch artists. Afterwards, enjoy a beer (or something else) at Café Hoppe, a proper Amsterdam local.

Van Dijk & Ko

Papaverweg 46, 1032 KJ (Noord), vandijkenko.nl

In a gigantic warehouse on the Noord side of the river IJ, you'll find an inspiring collection of refurbished second-hand furniture, tableware, and other beautiful items for your home (or beyond). Very noticeable is their wonderfully colourful Hungarian collection. There's surely still room in your bag for something to take home, isn't there?

Antiekcentrum Amsterdam

Elandsgracht 109, 1016 TT (Centrum), antiekcentrumamsterdam.nl

The largest covered antique shop of the Netherlands is housed in an old Peugeot garage. You'll find unique objects in all styles, from Art Deco to contemporary vintage. The shop covers an impressive 1,750 m2, so you can wander around for hours and feast your eyes. The items can be a bit pricey; it's not your standard second-hand shop.

Affordable Art Fair

affordableartfair.com

A few times a year, Amsterdam hosts the Affordable Art Fair. This provides an opportunity for art lovers to explore and acquire affordable yet compelling artworks from both emerging and established artists.

↓ STRAAT MUSEUM

RECORD SHOPS

Concerto

Utrechtsestraat 54-60, 1017 VP (Centrum), concerto.amsterdam

They call themselves 'the greatest record store on earth', which could be considered a subjective statement. However, there might be an objective truth to it, since the extensive collection of Concerto is housed in not one, not two, not even three, but five separate – yet consecutive – buildings. Hours of browsing guaranteed. The coffee they serve is also quite good.

Distortion Records

Westerstraat 244, 1015 MT (Centrum), distortion.nl

If you don't mind digging for that one vinyl you want, head to Distortion Records. There's always something to tickle your fancy within the stacks of records that reach from floor to ceiling. Can't find what you're looking for? The friendly owner is more than happy to retrieve your record of choice.

Waxwell Records

Gasthuismolensteeg 8A, 1016 AN (Centrum), waxwell.com

Though small in size, Waxwell Records offers great diversity. You'll find brand new as well as second-hand vinyl in all genres, from pop to disco, and reggae to jazz. They usually have a small selection on sale – it's certainly your lucky day if the one vinyl you have been looking for is in there.

Rush Hour Records

Spuistraat 110, 1012 VA (Centrum), rushhour.nl

Go to Rush Hour Records if you want to find some new artists, albums, and genres. Feel free to use one of the available record players in the shop to give your newly found vinyl a listen before you proceed to the till. Good to know, they don't sell CDs.

SHOPS WE LOVE

Coppenhagen Kralen

Rozengracht 54,
1016 ND (Centrum),
coppenhagenbeads.nl

You'll find countless small jars with all colours of beads in the oldest bead shop of the Netherlands. From freshwater pearls to ceramic beads, to beautiful vintage clasps for necklaces. They also sell everything else you need to make your own jewellery. Looking for shelter on rainy days? They organise group workshops (for four-plus participants). Your own handmade jewellery as a souvenir.

↓ HET MUIZENHUIS

Het Muizenhuis

*Muntplein 8, 1012 WR
(Centrum), sam-julia.com*

This shop, or museum, is a feast for the eyes. The little worlds in here were originally sets made for *The Mouse Mansion* children's books. Everything you see is handmade, down to the smallest details, such as the iron, calendar, and even cutlery. An Amsterdam family opened their first shop in the Jordaan. In 2023, as they were growing in popularity, they moved to the city centre into this large two-story building. The books about the Amsterdam mice have been translated into 27 languages, and a television series is in production.

Schaak en Gowinkel Het Paard

Haarlemmerdijk 173, 1013 KH (Centrum), schaakengo.nl

This game shop, a staple in the world of strategic board games, has been around for years. Beautiful chess sets, Japanese games, puzzles, or other fun games: you'll find everything you'll ever want. On sunny days, they put out seating for you to play chess.

Lambiek

Koningsstraat 27A, 1011 ET (Centrum), lambiek.net

Lambiek was Europe's very first comic shop. They opened in 1968, possibly even making it the oldest in the world. You will feast your eyes on the impressive collection of comics in every genre.

Het Oud-Hollandsch Snoepwinkeltje

Tweede Egelantiers-dwarsstraat 2, 1015 SC (Centrum), snoepwinkeltje.com

This sweet shop takes you back in time: this is what confectioneries looked like in Amsterdam in your great-grandmother's time. Nostalgically fill your own paper cone with the tastiest liquorice and sweets.

GREEN AMSTERDAM

PARKS AND SWIMMING

Amsterdam has plenty of green spaces to enjoy. During the summer months, temperatures are normally quite comfortable but there will always be days when it gets humid and plainly too hot. Don't forget to pack your swimwear if you want to take a dip!

PARKS

Oosterpark

The perfect green oasis for a picnic or walk. There is no swimming at Oosterpark, but there is plenty of shade. Grab some snacks from nearby Dappermarkt or one of the shops along Eerste van Swindenstraat or Javastraat and enjoy a few lazy hours. Take tram 1 or 3 and get off at Beukenweg.

Oosterpark, 1012 AA (Oost)

Amsterdamse Bos

On the southern side of the city, you'll find these stunning woods. At three times the size of NYC's Central Park, you can easily spend a few hours walking around, taking in the greenery. Or you could rent a canoe and explore the area from the water. From train station Amsterdam Zuid, hop on bus 358 and get off at Amsterdamse Bos.

kanoverhuur-adam.nl, amsterdamsebos.nl

Flevopark

This large park in Oost, on the outskirts of the city, is worth visiting to escape the crowds. You can head to nearby Flevoparkbad for a refreshing dip. Take tram 3 or bus 37 to get there. Within the park, there's a small distillery where you can sample homemade liqueurs, bitters, and gins. Opened only

during the summer months, starting from April.

Flevopark 13a, 1095 KE (Oost), nwediep.nl

Sarphatipark

A pleasant park in De Pijp, where young families gather on sunny days. It's a centrally located city park perfect for taking a break. Grab a Surinamese sandwich to go from Tjin's Toko at Eerste van der Helststraat 64 if you're feeling peckish.

Sarphatipark 37I, 1073 CP (Zuid)

Vondelpark

Undoubtedly the most famous park, loved by locals and tourists alike. In this expansive park with multiple entrances, you can relax on the grass bringing along your own packed lunch, snacks, and drinks. Or you could take a seat on the terrace of Proeflokaal 't Blauwe Theehuis.

Vondelpark 5, 1071 AA (Zuid)

Erasmuspark

The design of this small yet charming park in West is inspired by the paintings of Piet Mondrian. You're allowed to barbecue on the large open field, but just strolling through the park is pleasant too. Take tram 13 or bus 18 from Central Station.

Erasmuspark 1, 1056 LE (West)

Westerpark

This sprawling park located in West offers plenty of space. Nearby Westergasterrein has a lot to offer in terms of events and entertainment. From festivals to performances, there's always something on. Take bus 21 or 22 from Central Station.

westergas.nl

↓ SARPHATIPARK

↓ WESTERPARK

↓ OOSTERPARK

↓ VONDELPARK

SWIMMING

Marineterrein

In the middle of the city centre, this popular swimming spot is always buzzing. Go there to see and be seen! Bring your own drinks and enjoy the vibe. And the catwalk.

Kattenburgerstraat 5, 1018 JA (Centrum)

Entrepotdok

A truly unique swimming spot situated next to Artis Zoo. Don't be surprised if you hear or even see one of the animals while you're there. Facing Bloem eten & drinken, turn right. Cycle along the boardwalks and take a seat wherever you'll find a space.

Entrepotdok 36, 1018 AD (Centrum)

Noorderparkbad

In this charming, modern public swimming pool you will certainly have a great time. Take metro 52 to Noorderpark and walk through the park to get to the pool.

Sneeuwbalweg 5, 1032 VS (Noord), amsterdam.nl/noorderparkbad

Zeeburgerkade

Cruquius is one of Amsterdam's newest waterfront neighbourhoods. Here, you can take a plunge into the river IJ from the boardwalk. Go to Wijnsilostraat and head towards the river to find this spot. Afterwards, enjoy a drink at KRUX Brewery.

Cruquiusweg 83D, 1019 AT (Oost), krux.nl

Sloterplas

This urban beach is perfect to seek relief on hot days. It's a bit outside the city centre. Take tram 13 from Central Station, get off at Burgemeester Reindopstraat and walk for about ten minutes. **Sloterplas Strand, 1064 GW (West)**

Bogortuin

A popular gathering spot in Oost where youngsters as well as families enjoy the lively atmosphere and seek refreshment in the water. You can take a slightly deeper plunge from the quay. A perfect summer day is guaranteed. Take bus 43 from Central Station towards Borneo Eiland.

Bogortuin 60, 1019 PG (Oost)

↓ AMSTEL

VEGETARIAN AND VEGAN AMSTERDAM

Gartine

Nestled in an alley between the bustling Kalverstraat and Rokin, you'll find this delightful breakfast and lunch spot. Many of the fruits and vegetables used are grown in their own allotment in the Beemster area, just outside the city. You can really taste the care and attention they put into each dish.

Taksteeg 7, 1012 PB (Centrum), gartine.nl

SLA

The salads from organic salad bar SLA offer surprisingly delicious flavour combinations, and they're generously sized, perfect for sharing. You can dine in or take your meal to go and enjoy it in a nearby park.

Westerstraat 34, 1015 MK (Centrum), ilovesla.com

Bloem

A unique spot on the tranquil eastern side of the city centre, by the water, where you can enjoy a vegan lunch or dinner. They offer sandwiches, flavourful soups, and delicious pastries. Simple and tasty, that's all we need, right?

Entrepotdok 36, 1018 AD (Centrum), bloem36.nl

Madre

A fantastic spot in the Jordaan, where plant-based Mexican dishes are served in a relaxed atmosphere. Our favourites? Guacamole (freshly prepared at the table!), cauliflower in chipotle sauce, and mushroom *ceviche*. The cocktails are excellent too.

Westerstraat 186, 1015 MR (Centrum-West), madre.amsterdam

Helin's Vegan Döner

Vegan döner isn't commonly found. However, the plant-based döner in this Turkish shop is tender and tasty. They also offer sandwiches with 'regular' döner meat.

Linnaeusstraat 221, 1093 EP (Oost), helinsdoner.nl

Abu Amr Koshari

Divine Egyptian street food called *koshari*, generously filled pitas with options like vegan feta, and plenty of vegetables. Top it off with tahini sauce. Take away only.

Eerste Oosterparkstraat 91, 1091 GW (Oost), abu-amr.nl

The Meets

Where to begin? The decor at The Meets is tasteful, there's plenty of colour without it being overdone, their service is very attentive, and the dishes are beautifully presented. Almost too pretty to eat, and the flavours complement each other very well. Very much worth the visit.

Sumatrastraat 28, 1094 ND (Oost), themeets.nl

Yemayá's Vegan Corner

A bit out of the city centre, but this small eatery is worth the trip. They serve delicious vegan versions of traditional Surinamese dishes such as *roti rolls* and *pom* sandwiches (*pom* is made from a root vegetable that grows in South America).

Reigersbos 3A, 1106 AP (Zuidoost), Insta @ yemaya.estate

d&a hummus bistro

A wide variety of hummus dishes, perfect for sharing. Always served with homemade pita bread, pickles, and small salads. You can also opt for a hot *shakshuka*: an egg dish in tomato sauce. All three locations offer a relaxed living-room atmosphere.

Maasstraat 72, 1078 HL (Zuid), dna-hummusbistro.com

Robin Food Kollektief

Hidden within a squatted former school, you'll discover this foundation run by volunteers dedicated to affordable healthy eating. The daily changing three-course menu is 100% vegan. They operate a social and activist kitchen, inviting you to come in and find out.

Frederik Hendrikstraat 111A, 1052 HN (West), robinfoodkollektief.nl

Dr. Falafel

Considered by many as the best falafel in town. In this small takeaway, you can get delicious homemade falafel pitas filled with generous portions of vegetables. The pitas are golden brown and delightfully fluffy. Treat yourself! (Closed on Sundays.)

Nassaukade 900, 1053 LV (West),
Insta @drfalafelamsterdam

NON-FOOD

Ecomama Hostel

Colourful and thoughtfully decorated hostel featuring vintage and fair-trade materials. With a shared kitchen. Relaxed atmosphere with a very good price-quality ratio. But bring earplugs, just in case.

Valkenburgerstraat 124, 1011 NA (Centrum),
ecomamahotel.com

Six and Sons

The 'Sons' in their name stands for 'Save our nature story', and with that mission, it is a wonderful destination for conscious shopping. You'll find clothes, food, home decorations, and more. Their brands share their sustainable stories. In the shop is a cocoa bar serving fair-trade drinks.

Haarlemmerstraat 41, 1013 EJ (Centrum),
sixandsons.com

Het Faire Oosten

An enormous shop in Oostpoort shopping centre with a name that's a play on *het Verre Oosten* (the Far East) as well as Fair Trade. Here, sustainable creators and entrepreneurs gather under one roof. In addition to clothes from ethical brands, you can find body care products, candles, cookbooks, stationery, and homeware.

Waldenlaan 208, 1093 NH (Oost),
Insta @hetfaireoosten

OUTSIDE OF AMSTERDAM

There are plenty of enjoyable options if you want to get out of the city. How about canoeing in green surroundings, relaxing at the beach, or visiting the beautiful cities of Leiden and Haarlem?

Zandvoort aan Zee

visitzandvoort.nl

This beach town is only half an hour from Amsterdam Central Station. It can get a little crowded during the summer months. Just walk a little bit further out and the crowds will slowly dissipate. A perfect spot for a nice long stroll along the shore all year round. There are plenty of good restaurants and beach clubs along the boulevard. Try Noosa or Kayuca during the summer months and Tijn Akersloot in winter.

Bloemendaal aan Zee

visitzandvoort.nl/ bloemendaal

Zandvoort's neighbour, another wonderful and popular seaside destination with even more great restaurants and clubs. Check Woodstock for a good festival vibe in summer. Republiek, for a very classy drink or a pizza, and San Blas, for tasty (vegetarian) snacks, are open all year. Take a train to Haarlem and then hop on bus 81.

IJmuiden aan Zee

ijmuiden.nl/en/beach

This expansive beach is a lot quieter than Bloemendaal and Zandvoort, with fewer beach clubs, and it is a bit more challenging to reach by public transport. It's a popular spot for kite and wind surfers. From Sloterdijk Station (West), take bus 382 towards IJmuiden aan Zee.

Muiden

muiderslot.nl, pampus.nl

This small, fortified town lies east of the city and is truly worth a visit. Step back in time at the medieval castle Muiderslot and Forteiland Pampus. The island is accessible by ferry.

Holysloot & Broek in Waterland

Dorpsstraat Holysloot 22, 1028 BD, holyboot.nl laagholland.com/waterland

Are you looking for peaceful nature? Two idyllic villages in the polder north of Amsterdam are easily reachable by rental bike. In Holysloot, you can rent a boat or canoe to explore the area from the water.

Haarlem

Spaarne 16, 2011 CH Haarlem, teylersmuseum.nl, visithaarlem.com

Haarlem, the provincial capital of North Holland, is a beautiful city with a charming historic centre to explore. Besides lots of unique boutiques and quirky shops, there is an abundance of terraces on the market square and along the river Spaarne. The city also has plenty of cultural offerings. Teylers Museum, the oldest museum in the Netherlands, is a must-visit. There, you can marvel at history, science, and art. Or visit Frans Hals Museum, dedicated to one of the finest portrait painters of the 17th century. Haarlem is only twenty minutes by train. Even its station is a sight to behold. For lunch, by LIMA is very nice and for dinner, nothing beats a good pizza at Nolita.

Volendam

vvvedamvolendam.nl

Head to Volendam if you want to immerse yourself in typically Dutch traditional culture. The fishing village is known for its old Dutch charm. You can pose in traditional Dutch costume — yes, including clogs — enjoy some raw herring, and stroll along the harbour. You won't be the only visitor, but you'll have a fun time.

Geitenboerderij Ridammerhoeve

Nieuwe Meerlaan 4, 1182 DB Amstelveen, geitenboerderij.nl

In the middle of Amsterdamse Bos, you'll find this little goat farm. At Ridammerhoeve, you can feed the goats. It is a lot of fun for children but seriously enjoyable if you're older too. In the farm shop, you can indulge in delicious homemade ice cream and other tasty products. And a visit to Amsterdamse Bos is a great idea in itself.

Leiden

visitleiden.nl

Not a big tourist destination, the charming city of Leiden, a small student town nestled between Rotterdam and Amsterdam, boasts stunning canals and historic buildings. Take a leisurely stroll through the old town and get lost in its hidden courtyards. Visit a couple of fine museums like Lakenhal and Naturalis, then wrap up your day at wine bar Goeswijn or Bar Lokaal.

If you travel by train via Haarlem in March and April, you should catch a glimpse of the blooming tulip fields along the way, turning your journey to Leiden into an even more rewarding experience.

INDEX

ABOUT THE AUTHOR

Iris Brans

Iris is an Amsterdam-based editor who has worked for several newspapers and (online) magazines, both local and national. She has also worked for local radio station AmsterdamFM. She settled in the city during her journalism studies and knows it like the back of her hand, having lived in all its districts – even on a houseboat opposite Central Station. In addition to her own favourite spots in (and outside) the city, she rallied her friends to bring in more suggestions, making this guide a collaborative effort. With this, Iris hopes that you'll have a splendid time in Amsterdam. Chances are you'll spot her at one of the snack bars or traditional bars from this guide. Come and say hi if you do!

WHY SHOULD I GO TO AMSTERDAM
the city you definitely need to
visit before you turn 30

Published in 2024 by mo'media
P.O. Box 359, 3000 AJ Rotterdam,
The Netherlands, momedia.nl

Concept
mo'media

Text and address selection
Iris Brans

Art direction and illustration design
Jelle F. Post

Editing
Ezra van Wilgenburg

Photography
Jelle Oostrom, Petra de Hamer,
Iris Brans, Nathalie Kloosterman,
mo'media BV, and others

Special thanks to
Maaike van Steekelenburg, Ruben
Kuipers, Nathalie Kloosterman, Eva
van den Berg, Lotte Leeuwis, Stefanie
Koumiotis, Sarah Berends, Noortje
Kuipers, Max Aronius, Anne Bakker,
Aniek van Someren and Hielco Kuipers

Why Should I Go To Amsterdam
ISBN 978 94 93 338 432
NUR 510

Disclaimer
The points of interested mentioned in this
travel guide have been selected by the author.
None of them have been paid for inclusion in
this book: the *Why Should I Go To* book series
is entirely ad-free.

Publisher's Note
Every effort has been made to ensure that
the information in this book is accurate at
the time of going to press. The publisher
welcomes any information or suggestions for
correction or improvement. Please send us
an e-mail at info@momedia.nl or a DM on
Instagram.

 whyshouldigoto

WHY SHOULD I GO TO?
Information on all our travel guides
on **WHYSHOULDIGOTO.COM**

**Why Should I Go To travel guides are available
for the following cities:** Amsterdam, Antwerp,
Barcelona, Berlin, Copenhagen, London, Paris,
and Prague. More cities will be added soon.
Check our socials for updates.